KEEPING Christ CENTER STAGE

Keeping Your Music Ministry in Check

WRITTEN BY

ANGELA L. BRYANT

Author: Angela L. Bryant
Cover Design: Dave Cavins of Razor Edge Studios
Page Design & Layout: Oseyi Okoeguale
Editor: Atlanta Literary League

Keeping Christ Center Stage

© 2013 by Angela L. Bryant & Sounds 4 the Soul Ministries.

Scripture quotations unmarked
are from the Holy Bible, King James Version

Scripture quotations marked NIV
are from the Holy Bible, New International Version

Scripture quotations marked ESV
are from the Holy Bible, English Standard Version

Scripture quotations marked AMP
are from the Holy Bible, Amplified Version

Scripture quotations marked NLT
are from the Holy Bible, New Living Translation Version

All Definitions are from the Webster Dictionary.

Table of Content

My Gratitude

How can I say thanks
for the things you have done for me
Things so undeserved
Yet you gave to prove your love for me
The voices of a million angels
Cannot express my gratitude
All that I am or ever hope to be
*I owe it all to Thee—**Andre Crouch***

I thank God for trusting me with this awesome but humbling task. As a result of writing this book, He has spiritually stretched me and reminded me of my role in His mission to save the lost.

In fact, in my quest to complete this assignment—writing this book—I was speaking with another Christian artist about his experience in ministry. Long story short, his testimony became my epiphany! Who knew?! What he shared was that when God revealed to him that his singing ministry was *not* his purpose but the *tool* God was using to complete the mission—spreading the good news of Jesus Christ—his whole perspective changed for the better. No longer was he concerned about driving the direction of his music ministry, but rather, allowing the Holy Spirit to lead. What a liberating realization for him, and what a revolutionizing ministry moment for me. ***To God be the glory!***

From My Heart to Yours

Thank you! Thank you for taking your ministry seriously—for wanting it to be more than frivolous entertainment. You deserve *huge* kudos for deciding to read this book when you could easily be doing something less productive (I say this with a smile), like watching a reality TV show of *someone else's* life or trying to mimic the stage presence and vocal acrobats of some of your favorite artists on BET, VH1, MTV or even TBN. But I am not judging anyone—that would be the pot calling the kettle black.

So, give yourself a pat on the back for taking this journey with me towards a Spirit-led, Christ-centered ministry.

And from my heart to yours, may the God of your music ministry bless you, direct you and *forever* be with you!

Dedication

I dedicate this *work of heart to*:

- all my Christian brothers and sisters currently and upcoming in the music industry. I know how difficult it is to sustain your ministry without compromising to keep it "relevant" in today's crazy world of music, especially in the Christian sect. I pray this book will inspire you to be *true* to the mission which God has called you. Remember, Jesus *never* compromised His mission and neither should you. You are the reason I wrote this book.

- to Earl, who often encouraged me to follow my passion—music ministry—when I would grow weary and discourage in its pursuit. Also, thank you for holding down the fort while I took a sabbatical week in Florida where I penned the first draft of this book. I couldn't have done it without the peace in knowing you had my back, and I appreciate you for it.

- my children, Sydni and Roderick (I miss you. R.I.P.), you are my inspiration...two of the reasons I push past my insecurities, fears and all that life throws at me to pursue and live out the purpose God has for me. May this book be a reflection of the God I've committed to live for and serve up to my last breath. I love you deeply!

- my parents, Henry and Dorrie Bryant who convinced me to always let God lead me in *everything* I do. This book stems from the spiritual teaching that you instilled in me. I love you!

- Ms. Gwen Dozier for inviting me to her life/business coaching session, January 2012, where she challenged me to write this book. What a remarkable woman of God. You amaze me!

- And last but not least, my extended family— Carmen Calhoun, Luvon Dungee IV, Larie Gray, Angela Green, Elise Hines, Susan Shell, Kiisha Paris-Smith, Donald Thoms, and David Williams—for keeping it 100! Throughout our relationship, I have grown so much as a result of your heart-felt honesty, love, loyalty, laughter, constructive feedback (that sounds better than setting me straight. lol!), and powerful prayers. You mean the world to me!

Foreword

I have found over the years that it is overwhelmingly easy to put self into the center of everything, including ministry. I mean, oftentimes, we do things for others so we can feel better about ourselves. We might help a hungry stranger and then go on television to brag (not testify) about helping hungry strangers. Or maybe we have rushed to the bedside of someone we were told was very ill and when we finished "ministering" to that person, we told everyone how nobody even bothered to visit until *we* visited. My two illustrations may not apply to you specifically, but I think you can see my point: We have all seen Mr./Ms. Self-orchestrating ways to become the center of attraction. We have seen it in our churches, on radio and television, in magazines and on the Internet, etc. And if you are less susceptible to this reality, praise God that you are learning to decrease, so He might increase.

I had the privilege of meeting Angela just more than 19 years ago at church. As I experienced her ministry, it became clear that we absolutely had to partner for the purpose of leading others to Christ. I am an author who sings, and she is a singer who writes (grossly oversimplified). Both of us desire that whatever we do, we keep God in the center. She even obliged me many years ago to create a joint evangelistic tract that has been passed along to people around the country to honor our Savior and His love for us. She's invited me to share on stage at some of her most pivotal ministry endeavors, and I was delighted to have her co-host one of my Christian talk program episodes. I am not sure whether godly friendship is key to our collaborative ministry, or collaborative ministry is key to our friendship, but I know that God has been front and center through it all, no matter what. I am honored to share one more time.

This brings me to the purpose of my writing here: The candor and honesty with which Angela wrote this book, is akin to that which she displays in reality (and I know, because we are great friends). Don't be confused by what I just said. Let me illustrate the point another way: Question—Is Angela's music ministry the perfect model of a Christian music ministry? Answer—Irrelevant! I hope you got that. The tenor of this book causes us all to come face-to-face with the startling revelation that ministry, no matter in what form, is not about us; it's all about God. That is not to say that how we live is irrelevant. Do not get me wrong. It is to say, however, that our focus in life and ministry is not whether or not we perform the prescribed duties perfectly. The focus is Christ, His incredible power to change us from the inside, so we can speak for Him on the outside. Ministry, Christ-centered ministry, is about submission to God's plans for our lives, and simply allowing those plans to shine through us, so others may do the same. The focus of all holy ministries is taking our marching orders from the Captain of our souls, which can only be done when we continually receive His living Spirit, by faith.

This book challenges us all to live holy in order to be effective ministers. However, if we encounter some area of lack, Angela does not leave us to lament and die in our weaknesses. Rather, she offers a hand up as a fellow minister who has to do regular spiritual gut-checks herself. She gives practical and relevant to-dos as simple guidelines. Oftentimes, projects such as these are pie-in-the-sky pep talks. I suppose there is a place somewhere for those, but *Keeping Christ Center Stage* brings all of us ministers, no matter the area in which we minister, back down to planet earth to diligence in service. She offers various exercises, checkpoints, challenges, and a sacred space for alone time with God, that all culminate to help us get a clearer perspective on the *how* of moving from point A to point B along our ministry journey with God.

I would be remiss were I to neglect to ask you a series of thought questions as you prepare to embark upon this spiritual journey with our sister minister Angela: If God can use anyone to accomplish His will, why did He choose you, at your job; in your home; at your doctor's office; in the 15th section of tenors of a 200 member mass choir; in your housing development; on television; at church; in prison; on that pulpit; in the homeless shelter; on the road with someone needing help with a flat tire? Why you? Why there? Why at that time? Is it because you were the best person for the job? Is it because you were more committed than others? Could He trust you more? Or is it for some other reason? I think the Bible has provided the clearest answer possible. Here it is: "For thou art an holy people unto the Lord thy God: the Lord thy God hath chosen thee to be a special people unto himself, above all people that are upon the face of the earth. The Lord did not set his love upon you, nor choose you, because ye were more in number than any people; for ye were the fewest of all people: But because the Lord loved you, and because he would keep the oath which he had sworn unto your fathers, hath the Lord brought you out with a mighty hand, and redeemed you out of the house of bondmen, from the hand of Pharaoh king of Egypt" (Deuteronomy 7:6-8).

I suspect that this project became a minister even to Angela's soul. If you are being saved out of spiritual slavery, sanctified, and filled with the Holy Ghost, lift up your voice and pray that the Lord will reveal His power so incredibly through this project, that you will be forever inoculated against self-focus and allow His effulgent light to shine brightly from the center of all he entrusts you to do for the saving of souls. Amen.

*L. **David Harris** is an editor, public speaker, voiceover artist, freelance writer, and author with more than 20 years of professional experience. His passion is to use words and technology responsibly as effective agents of change, the world over. As such, he considers any contribution he makes in these ways a privilege.*

INTRO

Center Stage:
the main focus of attention

As a Christian singer for more than 40 years, I personally know what it feels like to struggle with self-exaltation, self-glorification, and compromise in exchange for alleged success. In my heart, I knew my purpose was to sing for God's glory, but my flesh wanted more—more worldly recognition, fame, and wealth; not because I innately hungered for those things, but rather, because I thought they were symbols of real success.

Earlier in ministry, I struggled with my gift. At one point, I searched for "success" the way the industry depicts it; I envied artists of the current time who were extremely popular and wanted to be like them at any cost. I spent and wasted so much time trying to change the gift that God gave me—rejecting what *He* designed.

So, every time I stood at the microphone, whether it was in the studio or in front of a live audience, I focused mainly on my appearance and performance rather than the Christ performing through me.

> **Side Note:** *In this book, the use of the word "perfor-mance" is equivalent to the word "ministering'" and is used interchangeably throughout this book.*

Looking at the gospel industry today, it is apparent to me that several Christian artists have this same struggle—placing and keeping Christ center stage in their music ministry. With all the stage props and stunts as well as the glamorous apparel that often outshine the God they are singing about, it's no wonder God's children (Believers) and the world have a difficult time identifying or seeing Christ in the Christian artist's performance. It seems the minute the artist stands center stage, is the same moment the artist asks Christ to exit the stage. And instead of bringing glory to God's name, He's been traded for world fame. *Father, have mercy on us!*

Now you may be asking, "What's wrong with a little showmanship if it helps you engage and keep the audience's attention?" And for a quick moment, I'm tempted to say nothing is wrong with it. But then I am gently, but firmly, reminded by the Holy Spirit that I am not the focal point, but Jesus Christ is. And according to Exodus 20:5, God is a jealous God and *will not* share His glory with anyone. And rightfully so, since He is the Creator and we are His creation. Therefore, no one, including me, has the right to exalt himself above Him. After all, wasn't that the mistake Lucifer, the Maestro of all musicians, made while in heaven? And I quote,

> *"I will ascend to heaven and set my throne above God's stars. I will preside on the mountain of the gods far away in the north. I will climb to the highest heavens and be like the Most High"* (Isaiah 14:13-14).

And we know where that landed him—a first-class ticket to Hell. Yikes! But if Lucifer's story isn't enough for you, let's take a look at what happened to Peter when He took His eyes off Jesus during a crucial time in his life.

In the Gospel of Matthew chapter 14, the scriptures say that after the great multitude was miraculously fed by Jesus, that Jesus instructed the disciples, including Peter, to get into the ship and cross over to the side while he dismissed the crowd. Here's how it is stated in the King James Version:

> 24 But the ship was now in the midst of the sea, tossed with waves: for the wind was contrary. 25 And in the fourth watch of the night Jesus went unto them, walking on the sea. 26 And when the disciples saw him walking on the sea, they were troubled, saying, It is a spirit; and they cried out for fear. 27 But straightway Jesus spake unto them, saying, 28 Be of good cheer; it is I; be not afraid. 28 And Peter answered him and said, Lord, if it be thou, bid me come unto thee on the water. 29 And he said, Come. And when Peter was come down out of the ship, he walked on the water, to go to Jesus. 30 But when he saw the wind boisterous, he was afraid; and beginning to sink, he cried, saying, Lord, save me.

I know what you are thinking. You're asking, "Why is this a problem?" Peter had a legit reason for taking his eyes off Jesus. Not only was he was distracted by all the commotion from the storm, but he was also scared! More the reason why Peter should have KEPT his eyes and mind ON Jesus. Look at how Ellen G. White states it in the book, *Desire of Ages p. 381-382:*

> Looking unto Jesus, Peter walks securely; but as in self-satisfaction he glances back toward his companions in the boat, his eyes are turned from the Savior. The wind is boisterous. The waves roll high, and come directly between him and the Master; and he is afraid. For a moment Christ is hidden from his view, and his faith gives way. He begins to sink. But while the billows talk with death, Peter lifts his eyes from the angry waters, and fixing them upon Jesus, cries, "Lord, save me." Immediately, Jesus grasps the outstretched hand, saying, "O thou of little faith, wherefore didst thou doubt?"
>
> Walking side by side, Peter's hand in that of the Master, they stepped into the boat together. But Peter was now subdued and silent. He had no reason to boast over his fellows for through unbelief and self-exaltation, he had very nearly lost his life. When he

turned his eyes from Jesus, his footing was lost, and he sank amid the waves.

There you have it! When we as Christian artists allow distractions (fear, fame, pride, self-exaltation, to name a few) to become our focus while ministering, the enemy is able to get us off our mission and, in some cases, sabotage the ministry effort completely. In addition, when we self-exalt, we rob God of his glory. And that is unacceptable for any Christian.

Being convinced that there is a self-exaltation epidemic among Christian artists today, I have written this book, with the help of the Holy Spirit. As a person who cannot turn away from an unresolved issue without at least trying to resolve it, this book is my humble effort to rectify a wrong, even if it only helps one person with their music ministry. I guess what I am saying, in the words of Kurt Carr, is *"Put Jesus Back!"* in our homes, schools, (and do I dare say it), churches, and Christian music.

Since you are reading this book, it's safe to assume that you are either a vocalist, musician, pastor in ministry, or maybe someone who just wants to make sure that whatever you do, you do it to the glory of God (1 Corinthians 10:31). So my question to you is, "What is the *Why* for what you do?" In other words, "what is the mission and motive that drives both your ministry and life?" And let me just say that your answer has to be something more than, "I love music or I love to sing or I love to play." When you started your music ministry, I'd like to think that it was because God called you to it. Yes, you had the raw talent that He gave you, but most importantly, you had a yearning in your heart to answer God's call and use your talent for His glory. And it is with this assumption that I write this book.

In the following pages, my prayer and hope is for you, the artist, to revisit your purpose and reason for being a Christian artist. In other words, let's examine why you do what you do and for whom you do it. I also hope that my written words will move you to look deep within your heart and soul and perform a ministry check. What are you checking? You are examining the condition of your ministry's heart (spirit), purpose (reason or drive), and mission (task).

Have you defined the ministry's divine mission? Are you connected to the Master of the mission? Do you know the potential impact your ministry can have on you and your audiences when Christ is the center of attention? These are just a few ministry check questions we will address in this book. In fact, it is my hope that by the end of this book, you are able to prepare and present a Spirit-led performance that will encourage and strengthen the spiritual lives of both you and your listeners.

For your convenience, this book includes a journal (Sacred Space) at the back of the book so that you can daily record your thoughts, to-do lists, ideas, revelations, epiphanies, spiritual growth moments, and even just to doodle, if it helps you think (smile). However you choose to use it, just use it, please. Take advantage of this space for it is a sacred space where you and God can commune.

As one Christian artist to another, I excitedly invite you to journey with me as I transparently share my struggles, setbacks, and successes of my commitment to place and **keep Christ center stage** in my music and in my life.

With that said, let the journey begin!

Reference Notes:

Ellen G. White; *Desire of Ages,* (Mountain View, CA; Pacific Press Publishing Association, 1940), 339

MINISTRY CHECK

While looking through sermon notes I jotted down over the past few years, I came across the following *10 Principles of Ministry* that I hope will help focus your ministry (forgive me for not remembering the name of the preacher):

1. The *foundation* of ministry is CHARACTER.

2. The *nature* of ministry is SERVICE.

3. The *motive* for ministry is LOVE.

4. The *measure* of ministry is SACRIFICE.

5. The *authority* of ministry is SUBMISSION.

6. The *purpose* of ministry is GLORIFYING GOD.

7. The *tools* of ministry are PRAYER and the WORD OF GOD.

8. The *privilege* of ministry is PERSONAL GROWTH.

9. The *power* of ministry is the HOLY SPIRIT.

10. The *model* for ministry is JESUS CHRIST.

MINISTRY CHALLENGE

Whether you have an existing ministry or getting ready to start one, I suggest you memorize or visibly post the above *10 Principles of Ministry* to use as a reminder, guide, and evaluation tool to help keep your ministry in check. During your examination, should you discover (and you will) that there are areas of your ministry that fall short, don't dismay! Lay it before God and allow Him to align it with His will. He will not disappoint!

Of all the music that reached farthest into heaven, it is the beating of a loving heart.

Henry Ward Beecher

CHAPTER 1

Define the Mission and Vision

❧··❧ ········ ❧·❧·❧··❧ ········ ··❧·❧

Where there is no vision, the people perish.
(Proverbs 29:18)

The text at the top of this page is one of my favorites. As an entrepreneur, it is essential to understand the mission and vision of the company, preventing waste of time and money on tasks and objectives outside the scope of the company's mission and vision.

As a seasoned person in music ministry, I know that it is also vital to know and understand the mission and vision God has for your ministry. Without them, your ministry will fail or continuously miss the mark. So before we go any further, let's define *mission* and *vision*.

According to the Webster Dictionary, the word *mission* is defined as *"a task or job someone is given to do."* And the word *vision* means, *"a clear idea about what should happen or be done in the future."* It should be crystal clear after reading both of these definitions why you, as an artist, must define your ministry's mission and vision. Without it, you will not have a clear path for your ministry, leaving you vulnerable to the attacks of your enemy—the Devil! And we can't have that!

And why should we? God has provided us with the perfect mission statement:

> *"Go ye therefore, and teach all nations, baptizing them in the name of the Father, and of the Son, and of the Holy Ghost. Teaching them to observe all things whatsoever I have commanded you."*
> (Matt. 28:19, 20a)

And He doesn't stop there. He also gave us the vision:

> *"But don't be so concerned about perishable things like food (money, apparel, and fame). Spend your energy seeking the eternal life that the Son of Man can give you."* (Luke 12:22)

In other words, we need not to worry about how we will survive during the mission. Instead, we should focus on the end result so that everything we do brings us closer to obtaining it.

Let me interject a personal experience to illustrate the above statements.

Prior to committing to full-time music ministry, I would frequently sing at church and other Christian related events, as well as occasional secular gigs that paid good money. On the surface, all seemed well. But anyone with spiritual discernment could sense that all was *not* well.

Although, it was very easy to memorize the great lyrics of a Christian tune, it was nearly impossible to live those words without having a close relationship with the God they described.

After years of singing without a sense of right motive or reason, I became discouraged and decided not to sing at all. At the time, it seemed like the right and honest thing to do since I wasn't living what I sang about—In other words, not practicing what I preached. So, I decided to stop singing until my life reflected the words I sang. See, I didn't want to be a hypocrite, and I didn't want to disgrace God's name.

It sounded like a good plan, but it didn't last long. Deep down, I knew God had called me to the music ministry, and I would never be at peace running from His call. At the young age of seven, He placed a burning desire in my heart to serve Him. And that desire, although at times barely smoldering, never died. Yes, there were some close calls where it looked like my passion for music had been extinguished by my preoccupation with other *stuff*; but God had a plan for my life, and He reminded me of that in 1999.

While working for a very reputable company and keeping myself preoccupied with other *stuff*, God allowed me to pen the words of the song that would strike a chord in the depth of my soul and change the course of my life forever. The name of the song is *Born with a Purpose (see lyrics below)*.

This song has proven to be one of the best songs I have written and recorded. Not only has it rekindled my commitment to the call God has on my life, but it has, also, inspired others. From the testimonies that I receive from people worldwide regarding this song, it is apparent that God is calling them to return to the abandoned call on their life as well.

After assessing my music ministry of more than 10 years, I am sad to say that earlier on it was not consistently Christ-centered. I lacked a true understanding of my ministry's mission, purpose, and vision. And as previously mentioned at the beginning of this book, it was not until I realized (thanks to an honest peer) that my vocal gift is not the *purpose,* but the *tool* God uses for the *mission,* that it all came together for me. Now that I understand that my *mission* is to use my vocal talent (singing and speaking) to spread the Gospel of Jesus Christ; I also understand that my *purpose* is to help souls come to know and accept Christ as their Lord and Savior, while also encouraging and fortifying believers. Also, it is apparent to me what the *vision* of the ministry looks like in the future.

Unfortunately, so many self-acclaimed (yes, I said it!) Christian artists do not get the *BIG* picture that God has for using their talents. Instead, they pretentiously perform song after song, concert after concert in the name of Jesus Christ. In place of God receiving the glory, they exalt themselves via savvy showmanship and glamorous apparel. You would think that the titles *"Christian Artist,"* *"Psalmist,"* and *"Singing Evangelist"* would be self-explanatory—a no-brainer—as to what their ministry should be. But when an artist is spiritually blind, they are vulnerable and weak in their ministry. How do you become spiritually blind and weak? By neglecting your relationship with God. This negligent course of action can only lead you to ministry failure and your soul's destruction.

MINISTRY CHECK

So what about you? Do you find yourself on a ministry roller coaster? One day you're riding high; other days, you are rapidly racing towards an ultimate low. Do you find there are performances when you are dead on but more times when you are just dead—spiritually dead to the will of God? In other words, is your ministry all about you?

If your answer is yes to any of the above questions, you are in a very dangerous place. But fear not! Where there is a will, there is a way, and "The Way" is none other than Jesus Christ (John 14:6).

You ask, "How does 'The Way' look?"

- First, "The Way" is clear of obstacles, pitfalls, and distractions that interfere with your relationship with God and diminishes the impact of your ministry.

- Second, "The Way" has no room for egos, including yours. Remember, Exodus 20:3 says, "thou shall have no other gods before me." After all, it's about Him, not us.

19

- Third, "The Way" exudes with Truth and Light of the one and only true God, never compromising it even in the face of fame and fortune.

- Fourth, "The Way" is scarcely traveled and rather lonely since its path requires self-denial and self-sacrifice.

- Lastly, but not least, "The Way" leads its travelers to *eternal life.*

If you have come to the realization that your ministry falls short of being Christ-centered, don't be discouraged. God has a plan for getting you back on track, and He's using this book to do it.

MINISTRY CHALLENGE

It is no secret that anything worth having doesn't come easy but involves hard work and effort. It's no different for ministry. Developing a Christ-centered ministry requires diligent effort on your part as an artist, and it all starts with a clear understanding of the mission and the vision. To get you started in the process, here are some suggested steps you must honestly and prayerfully complete:

1. Recommit your life to God vowing not to compromise the Truth or the Light of His Word.

2. As stated in Habakkuk 2:2, write down the mission, purpose, and vision God has given you for your music ministry and make it plain. Then and only then will you have a clear path to follow. Write 3 - 4 sentences for each.

3. Never compromise your mission for worldly fame and fortune. Its glory is short lived and unmatched to eternal life.

By implementing the above steps, your journey to complete the mission God has given you in His plan to save the lost while strengthening and encouraging the Saved has begun.

Once you have completed the above challenge, turn the page!

Born with a Purpose
written by
Angela L. Bryant

Verse:

When I look into the mirror, what is it I see?
Someone beautiful, unique, and that someone is me.
From the crown of my head, to the soles of my feet
God thoughtfully planned and designed a purpose just for me.

Chorus:

I was born with a purpose, perfectly designed
When God breathed life into me, He had a purpose in Mind
And though, I do not know my future, or what tomorrow brings
One thing I am sure of, I am a servant of the King.

Verse:

Do you worry about tomorrow, what the future holds?
Do you find yourself still searching, for that purpose, for that goal?
Trust not in your understanding, God has a plan for you.
In all your ways acknowledge Him, and you'll come to know it too.

Bridge:

Maybe, I'll be a missionary.
Or maybe a singer of His praise.
Or just a simple servant loving my neighbor
Whatever it may be one thing I know...yes, I know

(To purchase the single, *Born With A Purpose,* go to
Cdbaby.com/cd/angelatunes.)

DON'T JUMP AHEAD OF YOURSELF!

Did you complete the previous chapter's
ministry challenge?

If no, please go back and do so.

If yes, great job!

You can now move on to the next chapter.☺

The best, most beautiful and most perfect way that we have of expressing a sweet concord of mind to each other is by music.

Jonathan Edwards

CHAPTER 2

Connecting to the Master of the Mission

❖·❖·············❖·❖·◆·❖·◆················❖·❖·◆

*Seek the Kingdom of God above all else, and live
righteously, and He will give you everything you need.*
(Matt. 6:33, NLT)

Have you ever attended a presentation where the presenter spoke so vaguely and apparently was not well prepared or schooled on their topic? Not only are they sweating bullets and hoping no one notices, but their audience is having no fun and probably thinking "what a waste of my time". And the fact is, no one has time to waste.

Well, that is how it can be if an artist attempts to minister in front of an audience BEFORE connecting with Christ.

Spiritually they cannot deliver the message in its full power because they failed to plug into the Source. And although they may fool some of the listening audience, they won't fool all of it, "for spiritual things are spiritually discerned" (1Corinthians 2:14). The sad thing about it is the presenter (artist) doesn't realize they are shortchanging both the audience *and* themselves.

How do I know they know? Because for some time in my ministry, I, too, was guilty of cheating the audience and myself.

Typically in preparation for the day of performance, I would pray about what to sing and thoroughly prepare for it. But there was one particular time where I did not do the norm because I was only singing one song. So I thought, "No big deal. I'll just wing it." Not only did I fail to ask God what He wanted me to sing, but I chose a song I knew I could easily get by with since I failed to prepare thoroughly.

I am not going to say that I got up before the audience and totally flopped in my performance; that wouldn't be a complete truth. But what I will tell you is that I felt naked and extremely nervous because I had walked out on that platform without the covering of Christ. I alone had taken center stage and was relying entirely on my effort and experience. As a result, I was paranoid and overly concerned about making a vocal faux pas that the audience would detect, instead of being open to the work of the Holy Spirit. Thanks be to God, I finished the song without any apparent signs of dissatisfaction from the audience, but I said to myself that by God's grace, I would not be in that predicament again. I can honestly say, for the most part, I haven't been.

Just in case you missed the lesson learned, here it is. Having an inconsistent devotional life where one day you're on, the next day you're off; some days you spend quality time with God, while other days you hardly speak, can only result in a destabilized ministry.

It is no secret that communication, or the lack thereof can make or break a relationship of any kind. Consistent, honest communication is key to having a healthy, thriving relationship of any type.

So why do so many Christians falter in their prayer life?

My guess is that because of wrongful pride, cherished sin(s), and insecurities, to name a few, our prayer life suffers. In my experience, these three barriers, alone, have stifled the lines of communication in all of my relationships—God included!

As Christian artists, when we fail to develop an intimate and sound connection with the Almighty God, we not only risk diminishing the impact of our ministry due to our lack of authenticity, but we also limit both divine optimization and utilization of our God-given talent when ministering before people.

Now I am not saying that God cannot use someone who lacks a relationship with Him because He has and he does. But because He gives each of us a choice to serve or not to serve Him, *how much* He can use us is limited. That was the case with King Saul of Israel. Turn to 1 Samuel 10 and follow me.

Before Saul was crowned king of Israel, he was a very humble and cowardly man who, along with the children of Israel, didn't believe he could be king, But over time Saul convinced himself and the people that he would be a great king.

See, Saul was very handsome and regal in stature and gave the impression of a strong leader, but God knew differently. God, unlike man, looks at the heart (motive) versus the outer appearance of a man when determining godly character.

As Israel overcame each battle against their enemies, the nation grew more confident in King Saul's leadership— leadership that would later lead him down a path to self-destruction and national catastrophes as a result of him losing sight of God's mission, purpose and vision for the nation.

Shortly after defeating the Amalekites under God's instruction (1 Samuel 14-15), Samuel confronted King Saul with reproach from God. God had given King Saul specific instructions to destroy all the Amalekites, including the men, women, children, and animals. But at that point in Saul's reign, he had grown so arrogant and self-reliant that he felt comfortable enough to override God's commands. What a bad and sad call on Saul's part. But that is what self-exaltation will do to a person – lead you into self-destruction. And that is just what happened to King Saul in 1 Samuel 15:

17"And Samuel said, When thou wast little in thine own sight, wast thou not made the head of the tribes of Israel, and the Lord anointed thee king over Israel? 18 And the Lord sent thee on a journey, and said, Go and utterly destroy the sinners the Amalekites, and fight against them until they be consumed. 19 Wherefore then didst thou not obey the voice of the Lord, but didst fly upon the spoil, and didst evil in the sight of the Lord? 20 And Saul said unto Samuel, Yea, I have obeyed the voice of the Lord, and have gone the way which the Lord sent me, and have brought Agag the king of Amalek, and have utterly destroyed the Amalekites. 21 But the people took of the spoil, sheep and oxen, the chief of the things which should have been utterly destroyed, to sacrifice unto the Lord thy God in Gilgal. 22 And Samuel said, Hath the Lord as great delight in burnt offerings and sacrifices, as in obeying the voice of the Lord? Behold, to obey is better than sacrifice, and to hearken than the fat of rams. 23 For rebellion is as the sin of witchcraft, and stubbornness is as iniquity and idolatry. Because thou hast rejected the word of the Lord, he hath also rejected thee from being king. 24 And Saul said unto Samuel, I have sinned: for I have transgressed the commandment of the Lord, and thy words: because I feared the people, and obeyed their voice. ²⁵ Now therefore, I pray thee, pardon my sin, and turn again with me, that I may worship the Lord. ²⁶ And Samuel said unto Saul, I will not return with thee: for thou hast rejected the word of the Lord, and the Lord hath rejected thee from being king over Israel.

³⁵And Samuel came no more to see Saul until the day of his death: nevertheless Samuel mourned for Saul: and the Lord repented that he had made Saul king over Israel.

What a sad story! It breaks my heart that someone who had it all, threw it all away because they loved self more than God. But King Saul is not the only person who traded their eternal life in God for a fleeting life of this fallen world. Many of us make that gamble every day when we don't surrender our hearts to God *daily*. For some reason, we settle for temporal things (wealth, people's approval, etc.) over having eternal life and all it entails.

King Saul traded both his earthly and heavenly rewards when he blatantly disobeyed the mission God had assigned him. No longer did he have peace and joy while he lived. He not only had a miserable remaining reign as

King of Israel, but King Saul lost his sons, his life and went down in history as a King who failed his nation. I am sure that was not part of his vision as King of Israel.

By now I am hoping you get the point I am making. But just in case, let me make it plain. Although King Saul was anointed and initially successful as King, he failed the mission because:

- He allowed self-pride and ego to get in the way which led to his disobedience to God which resulted in God's rejection of him.

- He compromised the mission, purpose and vision that God gave him.

- He traded the way of *Truth* for a *lie* and *Light* for *darkness.*

- And he neglected to develop an intimate and genuine relationship with the Master of the Mission. It is this very misstep that resulted in the domino effect mentioned above. But it is, also, this very step that could have fortified both King Saul's leadership and the Nation of Israel.

Now did God use King Saul to carry out his plan? Yes! Was it short lived? Yes! Could Saul's story have ended differently? Definitely YES, if only he had chosen to cooperate with God completely and whole-heartedly. And the same applies to you and me.

As long as we connect and *stay* connected to the Master of the Mission, we will receive our instructions to complete the mission and purpose of our life.

So here is my point. Although Saul technically remained King of Israel until his death, his leadership power had diminished. He no longer had God's backing or power aiding him as king and therefore was less influential and ineffective as the leader of Israel. In fact, God's Spirit had diminished so much in King Saul's life that in desperation to receive a divine word from God, he turned to a sorcerer, a witch whom Saul had forbidden anyone to pursue or be punished by death. Saul summoned the sorcerer to conjure up the spirit of the long-deceased prophet Samuel. See where sin can lead you?

To bring it close to home, there were times in the history of my ministry when I felt like what King Saul must have felt after his rejection—distant, despaired, and disengaged

KEEPING CHRIST CENTER STAGE

from God and my audiences. Not because God rejected me, but because, like Saul, I rejected Him. I rejected God's will for my life so I could try things my way, only to mess things up horribly. Sound familiar? The scary thing about it is that if something spiritually hadn't changed within me when it did, both I and my ministry could have had the same tragic ending as King Saul.

One of my greatest fears is for Christ to return and not recognize me as one of His own. Wouldn't it be a shame if we, as Believers and Christian artists, were to lead souls to Christ only to realize that we, ourselves, are lost? It could happen. Matthew 7:22-23 reads, *"Many will say to Me on that day, 'Lord, Lord, did we not prophesy in Your name, and in Your name cast out demons, and in Your name perform many miracles and concerts [added emphasis]?' And then I will declare to them, 'I never knew you; depart from me!'"* By God's grace, this will not be my fate. And I pray that you will not let it be yours either.

MINISTRY CHECK

Enough about me, what about you? What's your story? How is your relationship with God? How much time do you spend daily in prayer and Bible study? Do you give God a chance to speak to you by being still and undistracted? Are there any unconfessed sins or other barriers blocking the communication between you and Him?

MINISTRY CHALLENGE:

For the next 10 to 15 minutes, prayerfully write down the obstacles, distractions, and other hindrances that keep you from committing to a daily devotion time with God. After writing your list, pray and ask God to give you the grace to manage and or eliminate each item. Then stand back and experience the power of God as it draws you nearer to Him—equipping you for a Christ-centered ministry and, even more importantly, a Christ-centered life.

> **NOTE:** *I recommend you repeat this challenge periodically. God will show you new areas you need to surrender to Him. After all, sanctification is an ongoing process.*

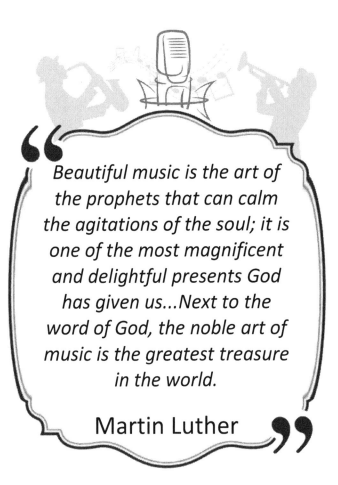

Beautiful music is the art of the prophets that can calm the agitations of the soul; it is one of the most magnificent and delightful presents God has given us...Next to the word of God, the noble art of music is the greatest treasure in the world.

Martin Luther

CHAPTER 3

Preparing for the Mission

❖◦◦❖◦◦◦◦◦◦◦❖◦◦◦❖◦◦◦◦❖◦◦◦◦◦◦◦◦◦◦◦◦◦◦◦◦◦◦◦◦◦◦◦❖

The soul of a lazy man desires and has nothing;
but the soul of the diligent shall be made rich.
Proverbs 13:4

A s I approached the microphone, my knees were very rickety, my palms a moisty mess, and my throat extremely dry—so dry that I thought I wouldn't be able to speak, much less sing. What was the problem? It wasn't a lack of experience, for I had been singing practically all of my life! But something was different this time. As the intro started to play, and as the very first singing measure approached, I realized at that moment what was wrong. I wasn't prepared! Yes, me—the professional singer—was not ready to perform much less prepared to minister.

37

I am ashamed to admit this, but sometimes I make the mistake of getting lax and unfocused when I do a task over and over again. The result, I come up short at the time of performance. This was one of those times.

It was a familiar venue (church) and audience type (Christian), but there was something different about the culture. To nicely put it, there weren't very many people who looked like me (African American) in the audience. I could count them on the fingers of one hand, including my assistant and me. But let me quickly say that their appearance or the lack of ethnic diversity wasn't solely the reason why it felt different to me. What made this audience different was that they appeared to be expressionless, disengaged, and they lived in the Midwest—Lincoln, Nebraska—that might explain their cold stares.

To make matters worse, I was trying out new songs that I hardly practiced. The audience was a *very* conservative crowd in every aspect—dress, beliefs, and music. Not that my style of music is edgy and very contemporary, but it definitely is not exclusively traditional or inspirational. And because I failed to research my audience, I was unprepared—not enough traditional and inspirational accompaniment soundtracks. The few songs that were fitting for this audience were new songs I hadn't practiced thoroughly; therefore, my performance was below par, and it showed.

There I was, standing before a group of people who appeared uninterested (at least that is what I thought), and it made me nervous! I knew and thought they knew, too, that I was not prepared to sing or minister to this audience, and that was not a comfortable situation. And although, at that moment, there was nothing I could do about their perception of me, there was something I could have done about my performance—prepared better!

Does the above situation sound familiar to you? Are you guilty of *winging it* too often? And do you find yourself needing to better prepare for all types of ministry engagements?

Well, I figured as much☺.

With that said, the remaining pages of this chapter spell out the checklist I created and use to prepare me for all ministry engagements.

KEEPING CHRIST CENTER STAGE

> **Disclaimer:** *This checklist is not law, and you should customize it to your ministry needs. The point is for you to create one and use it.*

ANGELA'S MINISTRY CHECKLIST

There are four components to my checklist:

1. Spiritual Readiness
2. Physical Readiness
3. Vocal Readiness
4. Performance Readiness

Let's explore each of them closely.

Spiritual Readiness

Right before I take the stage or platform, I make it a practice to spend some quality time in prayer. It is my way of ensuring that I have connected with the Source of my strength and talent and that I will be in His will when I take center stage. It is my sincere belief and personal experience that when I am not centered in Christ, I am spiritually naked, vulnerable, and unequipped to complete the task the way God intended. To say it another way, I have set myself up for failure when failure should not be an option. Okay, maybe not in showmanship but definitely in spiritual influence and God's complete utilization of me. More importantly, I risk missing out on an opportunity to experience the presence and nearness of God—the One I desire to know more intimately.

But I am not the only singer with this dilemma. Each time you and I take the microphone without Christ being the center of attention, we limit the Spiritual Power within us to reach and touch souls for Christ. I truly believe and understand that without Christ, I can do nothing but fail (see Matt. 19:26). But with Christ's strength, I can do all things (see Philippians 4:13).

Since Christ is the focal point of all faithful ministries, I offer you the following five tips—J.E.S.U.S.—to aid you in your daily pursuit of oneness with Christ while preparing you for His service:

J – Jumpstart your day with devotion and prayer. Confess any sin that could hinder the Spirit's full use of you.

E – Erase negative thoughts and feelings and embrace God's love for you every moment of the day.

S – Sing and speak praises to God throughout the day. This will help keep you connected and in tuned with God throughout the day.

U – Unite in spirit, body, and mind with the Holy Spirit, allowing Him to be your spiritual guide and cheerleader.

S – Serve God with all your heart in all you do, for "The heart service is what God requires; the forms and lip service are as sounding brass and a tinkling cymbal" (E.G. White, *Evangelism*).

Memorize the above steps and experience for yourself spiritual growth that will revolutionize both your ministry and life.

Physical Readiness

In my opinion, being physically fit seems to be a significant challenge for most people in America, I included. With television and radio bombarding our audio and visual spaces with lip-smacking, mouthwatering advertisements, it's no wonder Americans (kids included) suffer from obesity and other health-related issues.

As an amateur artist, you might think that being physically fit has little to do with singing. After all, you are only using your vocal cords, not running a marathon. Right? Wrong! Singing requires the support from your upper body, specifically your lungs, diaphragm, good posture, lips, tongue, ears, and let's not forget your brain.

Let me share a personal experience.

I had just completed a 30-minute set of passionate singing and speaking, not to mention, interacting with concert attendees and autographing CDs, when I realized how tired I was. Singing and meeting with people to encourage them and hear their testimony is rewarding. Stills it's also *extremely* exhausting, especially (you know what I am about to say) if you are not physically fit.

Now I don't claim to be the fittest person in the U.S.A., but I am no stranger to exercise either. I understand the link between physical fitness and vocal stamina. I remember the times when I was physically and vocally tired after completing a couple of songs. I'd have to take at least a minute in between songs before continuing. How pathetic is that?

But one day, the Holy Spirit convicted me in the area of temperance. So, in addition to changing my diet (I will address nutrition in the next section), I incorporated a 60-90-minute cardio and strengthening exercise regimen three to five times a week. Within just a few weeks, I noticed a difference in my vocal performance. I no longer needed to break in awkward places because I was able to sustain notes more easily. And all it took was a made up mind and a whole lot of grace from God to start treating my body, God's temple (1 Corinthians 6:19), the way it deserves to be treated.

Another major factor in physical readiness is sleep. I don't know about you, but when I am physically tired, I am of little use to anyone or anything, including singing. In fact, if I don't get at least seven hours of sleep, my speaking voice drops so low that I sound like Dorothy Zbornak from the "Golden Girls" television series (yes, I know I am dating myself). So, if my speaking voice needs an ample amount of sleep, how much more important is it that I get enough sleep to maintain my singing voice?

In case you didn't get it earlier, singing requires more than just your vocal cords. It also involves your lungs, diaphragm, brain, lips, and posture, to name a few. Consequently, when your body is fatigued and unable to function at optimal levels, the quality of your vocal performance and stamina is negatively impacted.

Therefore, it is highly recommended that a singer gets 7 - 8 hours of sleep on a regular basis. After all, rest does the body (and vocal cords) good☺!

I've covered a lot, so let's recap.

An artist who is serious about their music ministry will:

- incorporate an exercise regimen (after consulting with your physician) that works best for them,

- get 7 - 8 hours of sleep, and

- incorporate a diet that is vocal friendly (discussed in the next section).

When followed diligently, you will experience a much stronger performance as a result of increased stamina and healthier vocal cords, all of which lead to ministry longevity.

Remember, it's all about completing the *mission.*

Vocal Readiness

The vocal cord is a very delicate organ that, if not handled with proper care, can become severely, if not permanently, damaged. In some cases, singers have developed vocal nodules (a singer's nightmare) and were ordered by their physician to rest from all singing and speaking. In cases where the damage was very severe, surgery was required.

As a professional vocalist, it is non-negotiable to know your instrument and how to properly care for it. As a violinist, you would never leave your instrument out of its case and on the floor where it could be stepped on or its strings damaged or broken. So as a vocalist, you shouldn't haphazardly handle the health of your vocal cords. It will cost you loss of performance opportunities and revenue.

> *Side Note: If your occupation requires you to do a lot of talking on a regular basis, it is essential that you periodically take 10 to 15 minute breaks of complete silence throughout the day–allowing your voice to sleep, in a sense. Also, whispering is not an option because it overworks the vocal cord.*

So how do you take care of the vocal cords?

> **Disclaimer:** *Let me be clear when I say that I am not a professional trainer or voice professor, but I share personal experiences from my 35 years in music ministry.*

First, get professional training, if you haven't already. Unfortunately, some singers fail to do this and as a result, damage their vocal cords. I have read on countless occasions about singers (*i.e.*, Adele and John Mayer) who developed nodules and had to take a sabbatical from their singing career with hopes of being able to return to it. I am not saying that they didn't have vocal training, but applying what you know is even more critical.

Part of vocal training or practice is to warm up the vocal cords. Do not omit this vital step, or it may cost you more than the time it takes to perform it. Just as a runner must warm up and thoroughly stretch before sprinting down the track in order to avoid injury, so must a vocalist warm up and stretch the vocal cords to prevent vocal impairment. Working with an experienced vocal coach, who can teach you proper warm-up exercises suitable for *your* voice, will help keep your vocal cords healthy and properly functioning.

The amount of time needed to warm up will vary depending on the condition of your voice at the time of practice and the length of time you will be singing. For example, if you are expected to perform one song (averaging 4 - 5 minutes) and if your voice is in good shape (well-rested and hoarse free), then your warm up time could be anywhere from 20 to 30 minutes. And if your vocal cords are in poor condition due to hoarseness, but you must sing, I recommend that you *gradually* warm-up for 10 to 15 minutes to be sure not to overwork your vocal cords. WARNING: If at any time you experience pain, STOP IMMEDIATELY! (For more on hoarseness, please visit https://completevocal.institute/hoarseness/.)

Whatever you decide regarding vocal training, DON'T CHEAT and DON'T BE CHEAP! Invest in your gift and get professional vocal training. The return on your investment is guaranteed to outweigh its cost.

Secondly, be careful what you eat and drink. Many of us abuse our bodies with our poor eating and drinking practices and habits. I, too, am guilty of this more often than I like to admit, and boy, it can be painful. See, I suffer from acid reflux. So when I eat and drink certain types of food and beverages (i.e., tomatoes and caffeinated drinks), my body quickly lets me know that it is not happy. It sends damaging acidic fluid up my esophagus burning my vocal cords and leaving me hoarse for at least two days. So to maintain good vocal health, I've learned to monitor what I eat, in spite of what my taste buds crave.

So to wrap it up, let me say this. If you cherish your vocal gift, know what foods and drinks are not your vocal cords friends, and avoid them like the plague! So to wrap it up, let me say this. If you cherish your vocal gift, know what foods and drinks are not your vocal cords' friends, and avoid them like the plague!

The third vocal recommendation piggybacks off of the second. Limit or avoid dairy products altogether, especially a few days before a performance. This food type causes excessive mucus build up in the throat that can result in vocal inflammation.

> **Side Note:** *If you feel the need to clear your throat, DON'T! Doing so causes your cords to slam together and become irritated. If you must clear your throat, swallow hard (gulp) a few times.*

The fourth vocal tip to keep in mind is to stay hydrated by drinking plenty of room temperature water (drinking cold water is harmful to the vocal cords and stomach). As a singer you need to drink an average of 8 - 10 glasses of water a day, depending on your body weight. A simple way to determine the proper amount of water for your body is to divide your weight by 2. So, if you weigh 140 pounds, then you would need at least 70 ounces of water a day to keep you properly hydrated.

Other ways to help keep your vocal cords and surrounding mucous membranes hydrated are to:

- sip hot, decaffeinated teas. Industry experts recommend Marshmallow-root and licorice teas.

- avoid adding lemon juice to your water. It is known to cause throat dryness.

- steam your throat often by holding your head over a pot of hot water, placing a towel over your head and inhaling deeply for a few minutes.

- sleep with a humidifier especially the day before a performance in arid or very dry climates and seasons.

- avoid A/C when at all possible. It can dry out the air and your vocal cords.

- gargle with a mixture of warm salt water and a quarter-teaspoon of baking soda to help keep the vocal cords lubricated.

- limit alcohol and caffeine as well as antihistamines and menthol cough drops. These items also dry out the throat and irritate vocal cords.

By keeping your body properly hydrated, your vocal cords and the surrounding mucous membrane will be healthy and function correctly.

Last, but not least, avoid unnecessary screaming and shouting. You would think that this would be a "no brainer" for singers, but it's not, at least not with me. I am *SO* guilty!

As a mother, and as a driver in the DC Metropolitan area, I often find myself yelling, shouting, or screaming at my children and other incompetent drivers (hey, don't judge me...pray for me). But I am aware of the problem and am working diligently to fix it (smile).

In any case, I still must tell my peers that yelling is not good practice for someone who's serious about maintaining a healthy singing voice. And besides, it's not at all Christ-like. And isn't being Christ-like a part of the mission?

Performance Readiness

Although the prior three checklist items are very important in preparing for the mission, performance readiness is even more critical. Why? Your performance is what the audience will see. The other three tips are what happens behind the scenes or before curtain call. The actual performance is what the audience will experience and hopefully never forget.

The following are elements that help make a performance great or, at minimum, impressionable:

- A Christ-Centered attitude (humility).

- A reputable repertoire (biblically grounded).

- Appropriate attire and appearance (most people see you before they hear you).

- Engaging the audience (empathize and sympathize with the people).

A Christ-Centered Attitude is a spirit of humility and meekness. It involves denying self of exaltation and allowing the Holy Spirit to lead throughout your performance. God is to be glorified by songs of praise & worship from a pure heart filled with love, humility, and devotion to Him.

As I mentioned earlier in the book, in my opinion, artists struggle with having a Christ-centered attitude, and it's no wonder. With the many accolades and the extreme adoration, artists are showered with by people, it is no wonder their egos are easily inflated—squeezing out the Spirit (attitude) of Christ in your ministry. With that in mind, you must be very prayerful and anchored in the Word so as not to drift away from the course God has mapped out for your ministry.

A Reputable Repertoire is one that reflects the life and Gospel of Jesus Christ. EVERY lyric and chord of a song should exude the principles of Christ...love, peace, joy, hope, salvation, etc. If the message and the music don't point us to Christ and what He stands for, then it isn't Christ-centered. Point blank!

KEEPING CHRIST CENTER STAGE

Question. Would you wear a casual outfit to a formal affair? If you were to practice appropriate etiquette, the answer would be no. And why do you think that is? Could it be because it is considered a sign of disrespect to your host or that you would be the awkward one in the room? Or maybe it would be too much of a distraction, in a bad way. When building a repertoire or choosing a song for an engagement, you must be mindful of the audience who will receive it. Otherwise, it could turn out to be a non-engaging, awkward and even distracting and disappointing performance for both the singer and the audience; as a servant of God, we don't want that to be the case.

The following are steps I take to help me stay on the right track with song selections:

- *Know your audience.* By conducting a brief interview or having the host of the event complete a short questionnaire, I can surmise what type of audience to expect. Ask questions like, "Which would you consider your audience or congregation to be, conservative or contemporary?" and "Are there any music restrictions I need to know about, such as no drums or rhythm-type instrumentation?" Knowing your audience will help prevent a performance that will offend the listeners. Now I am not saying that you can please all of the audience, all of the time, but you can help reduce the number of people who are not pleased with your performance. Once you identify the audience type, you are able to select a suitable song(s) more easily. Why is this important? As I mentioned above, you want to avoid unnecessarily offending people, especially in ministry. *NOTE: There are times when the song or message you deliver will spiritually offend and/or convict the heart of a person. In those cases, it is a God thing, and there is nothing you can and should do about it.*

- *Check to see if there is a theme for the program.* If there is, search for songs in your existing repertoire that fit the theme both lyrically and musically (*i.e.,* conservative, contemporary) for your audience.

- *Pray for Spiritual Guidance.* Whether you are singing Christian or secular music, you always want God to give you peace about the songs you choose. Remember, you are a messenger of God, and someone is sitting in the audience who needs a specific word from the Lord through your song(s) and spoken word.

Appropriate Attire and Appearance is a sensitive and touchy topic with most people, including me. Nonetheless, it is an area that I feel compelled to address as it relates to Christian ministry.

Now, before you close the book and put it away in a drawer (or trash), please hear me out.

As a woman in music ministry, I have struggled in this area. Honestly, I like to look good, and I want others to find me appealing as well. Not that I want them to focus on my appearance, but I would be lying if I said that it wasn't some of my motivation in choosing what I wear. Years ago, I learned a hard lesson when I chose myself over ministry.

One week, I was invited to be the special guest artist for an early morning women's worship service held during their worldwide general conference. Being very familiar with the particular denomination, I knew its members were pretty conservative, as it is with most conservative and traditional denominations, especially when it comes to women's appearance. But for some self-centered reason, I chose to ignore this piece of knowledge. Since my performance was so early in the morning, I thought I could get away with being very casual, mainly since I had attended other women conferences in this denomination where the women dressed very casual for the worship services.

> *Side Note: The truth. I had underestimated my assignment since it wasn't during the main service where thousands of people would attend. I hate to admit it, but I viewed this particular engagement as a non-paying, insignificant gig; thus, it showed in my appearance.*

So the first morning I was to perform at the woman's worship service, I showed up in jeans, a casual top and flip-flops. I thought this was going to be an intimate assembly in a small room at the convention center. It would be quick, and I would slip out right after singing. Boy, was I wrong!!!

> **Yes, another Side Note:** *If I had done my homework regarding the event's specifics, this could have saved me from embarrassment.*

As I approached the room where the worship service was being held, I realized that it was not just one small room but several large rooms merged to accommodate several hundred women and men, even! I gasped at the sight of the stage, which was huge, beautifully decorated and ready to receive its participants. The atmosphere was absolutely amazing and the congregation was totally engaged in the worship service upon my arrival. Everything was fully prepared, except me! I was not appropriately dressed and dared not further embarrass myself, the program host, and, most importantly, misrepresent God. They trusted me with this assignment, and I failed them!

Now some might say that the host should have mentioned the dress code for the service, but I know it was my responsibility to ask about the attire before leaving home.

So, what did I do? I humbly (and full of embarrassment) apologized and asked to return the following morning dressed appropriately for the occasion. The host understood and agreed. So, I returned the next morning fully prepared, and God showed up and showed out. And I am happy to say that both the audience and I were blessed as a result.

Lesson learned!

I share this personal experience so that you will not make the same mistake I made—failing to be ready in appearance for ministry, regardless of the size of the venue and audience. This particular story ended happily. But what if the host had only scheduled me for a single performance versus an entire week? I would have missed the opportunity to minister, disappointed the host (who would probably never invite me back) and failed God in completing my assignment.

The above example is just one aspect of what it means to be appropriately dressed in ministry. My final aspect is this. Dress to impress! In other words, before you take the stage, make sure your appearance makes the right impression to your audience.

Stay with me.

It's safe to say that most people see a person before they get a chance to hear and know them. And unfortunately, people often draw inaccurate conclusions and perceptions about a person based on what they see. Call it unfair and judgmental, but it is what it is. And in ministry, it is no different.

When you arrive at the venue and as you take the stage or platform in preparation to sing, people are watching and drawing conclusions about you even before you say your first word or sing your first note. Their perception or story they create about you is based on what you are wearing (including makeup and adornment), how you are wearing it (or how it is wearing you) and the attitude with which you are strutting it.

I am not going to tell you another experience, but I will say this much. You can sabotage an opportunity to minister in a powerful way when your appearance contradicts your message.

How? Because some people are easily distracted by the slightest thing, the attention that God *should* be getting can be misdirected to the artist. In some cases, instead of the Son of God shining through the artist, the artist's outfit outshines the Son of God. Additionally, some people could regard the artist as a hypocrite and reject or not receive their ministry. To take it a step further, I am convinced that we dishonor God when we misrepresent Him with our appearance (on and off the stage), and this should never be the case with a ministry.

Ellen G. White was a prolific Christian author in the 1800s and early 1900s. She wrote about the following regarding a Christian's appearance in the book, *Gospel Workers*:

> *"The God of heaven, whose arm moves the world, who gives us life and sustains us in health, is honored or dishonored by the apparel of those who officiate in His honor... our words, our actions and our dress are daily, living preachers (sermons) gathering with Christ or scattering abroad"* (Page 173).

One way to avoid any misperceptions and distractions before, during, and after you minister is to just *KEEP IT SIMPLE.* And what I am saying shouldn't come as a surprise to a Christian. Apostle Timothy advised that "women (men) [emphasis added] should adorn

61

themselves in respectable apparel, with modesty and self-control..." (1 Timothy 2:9a, ESV). And this advice is achievable when you are prayerfully mindful of what you wear from head to toe, including makeup, fragrance, adornment, and even hairstyles.

Well, enough said! May the Holy Spirit continue to direct you.

There is one last, but definitely not least, component of *performance readiness.* While you are approaching center-stage and even before you speak or sing your first lyric, there is one element that must happen in the beginning, during, and after the performance—Engaging the audience.

Engaging the Audience—getting and keeping their attention—requires you to purposefully and intentionally connect with them. More importantly, it is essential that the Holy Spirit be allowed to flow freely through you via your words, songs and body language.

One of my pet peeves is to watch a presenter, regardless of the trade, halfheartedly try to tell, sell or convince me of something. To make matters worse, they are not well prepared to make the presentation, thus wasting my time and patience.

When an artist shows up to minister on God's behalf but lacks passion or authenticity in their performance, they lose the attention (that is if they ever really had it) of the audience. The unprepared performer not only risks people thinking they are not sincere, but they also short change the audience in receiving their spiritual blessing.

As an artist, it is important for you to pray that God will give you the spirit of compassion and love for the souls sitting before you so that you genuinely connect with the them.

Once you make the connection with your audience, you must sustain the connection by maintaining good eye contact. Facial and hand gestures should reinforce and emphasize what you are singing and talking about. People are prone to carefully listen when once convinced that you are presenting something they need, and you can vouch for it, which leads me to my next point.

Your testimony is the best tool you have to use in ministry. Regardless of how raunchy or embarrassing your story is, it is your life experiences and tests that give your ministry credibility. And that is why sharing it during your performance helps keep your audience engaged and open to receive what God has for them. Everyone likes a true story, especially one with a happy ending. So, share your testimony! Write it down! Pray about how to present it in the light of Christ. Through your story, let the world know that Christ is still saving souls, one testimony at a time!

We've covered a lot in the last several pages. So let's sum it up!

While you are a musical artist, do not assume that you do not need to prepare. Preparation is essential, regardless of the level of your talent. To take it a step further, when your music is your ministry, you must strive for excellence since you are representing a God of Excellence. Anything less would be shortchanging the mission.

Make it your obligation to be balanced spiritually *(connect to the Master of the mission)*, physically *(practice a proper diet, exercise regularly, get enough sleep)*, vocally *(practice daily, get professional training when needed, stay properly hydrated)*, and professionally *(have a reputable repertoire, wear appropriate attire, and engage the audience)*. In short, be ready before you stand center stage in the name of Jesus.

MINISTRY CHECK

Take a moment and think about your past few performances and consider how much prayer, time, and thought you put into preparing for it, especially if you categorized it as an insignificant occasion. Were you satisfied with the outcome(s)? Was there an area(s) *(spiritual development, vocal vitality, song selection, practice, etc.)* that could have used more time and attention in preparing for the performance? Did you approach each performance with a spirit of excellence, regardless of the size of the honorarium and or audience? Did you take time to gear up with prayer, a confessed heart, and a cloak of humility? And did you consult with the Holy Spirit on what to sing and say to ensure that the right message is delivered for that audience?

MINISTRY CHALLENGE

Before you commit to another engagement, create a schedule that allows you the time for daily devotion, proper physical, vocal, and performance preparation so that God will be glorified. Then prayerfully submit it to God, asking for His grace to implement it in your daily routine. Remember, you are gearing up for the spiritual battle, and you don't want to go unarmed.

Next, write your testimony and memorize it. It is one of the most powerful tools God has given you to use for His glory. So use it! And if you find yourself afraid, in the words of Joyce Meyer, "Do it afraid!" while remembering to "commit your actions to the LORD, and your plans will succeed" (Prov. 16:3, NLT).

Now get busy!

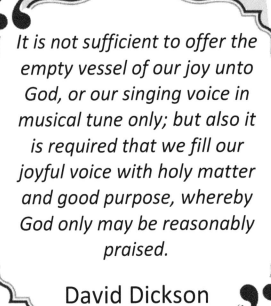

It is not sufficient to offer the empty vessel of our joy unto God, or our singing voice in musical tune only; but also it is required that we fill our joyful voice with holy matter and good purpose, whereby God only may be reasonably praised.

David Dickson

CHAPTER 4

Executing the Mission (Part I):
Keeping Christ Center Stage

━━━━━━━━━━━━━━━━━━━━━━━━━

Everyone who ministers before the people should feel it a
solemn duty to take himself in hand...and give himself to
the Lord...determined that he will have none of SELF,
but all of Jesus. (E. G. White)

U p to this point, the focus has been on adequately
preparing for the mission—*sharing the Gospel of*
Jesus Christ in song and testimony. Although this is a very
crucial, foundational step in building a Christ-centered
ministry, we must take it a step further in reassuring that
Christ remains the center of attention *while* we minister
before people.

Now before you shoot the messenger, let me just say that I am talking to myself first and foremost. As a Christian artist, I struggle with carrying out the mission, especially when I am not spiritually prepared. From what I have seen in other performances, I think it's safe to say that I am not the only one struggling with this.

"How can this be with a Christian artist?" you ask. Here's how.

When you think about it, it is easy for a singer to get into a routine or rhythm with vocal, physical, and performance training with little or no spiritual effort. But in order to successfully keep Christ center stage of every performance, you must be spiritually connected with God allowing His Spirit to work through you. But, again, let me be clear about what type of connection I am referring to— a personal relationship with Christ. In other words, whether there is a scheduled performance or not, you are determined that Christ is ALWAYS center stage in your life. And there are benefits to doing so.

A benefit of showing up to an event with a Christ-centered attitude is, you are able to handle anything that is hurled at you because Christ is with you. As you know, the enemy is always lurking around where authentic ministry is happening. So, showing up unarmed (see Ephesians 6:11) is not an option if you want to complete the mission successfully. Whether or not the host fulfills your expectations, you should not be deterred or distracted from completing the assignment God has given you. Be determined that nothing or no one will keep you from sharing the Good News of Jesus Christ and keep Christ the center of attention before, during, and after your performance.

Another benefit for being Christ-centered on stage is, God receives all of the glory; therefore, He uses you to draw all men unto Him, the Life-Giver, and that pleases Him. But when you attempt to exalt yourself in place of God— showcasing your talent and using showmanship to receive the glory—you sabotage the work of the Holy Spirit in and through you, thus God is not pleased. Our God is a jealous God (see Exodus 20:5) and commands that we not worship any other gods or idols, including ourselves. Service to our God requires humility and self-denial.

Blessings are another benefit of being Christ-centered on stage. Knowing you have done what God has asked you to do *His way* gives you a sense of peace and fills you with the joy of the Lord. What a blessing that is!

The audience is also blessed because you have allowed the Holy Spirit to use you to minister to their hearts and situations; so much so, they sometimes share their testimonies with you. Personally, this does my heart good. Knowing that God is using me to personally touch the lives of others for His purpose, glory, and honor reaffirms my call to the music ministry and encourages me to complete the mission.

I could go on and on listing the benefits because God's blessings are infinite. But, I'll pause and share why I choose to keep Christ center stage in my ministry:

When my work on earth is finished
And time shall be no more,
When Christ receives me to Himself
And gives me my reward,
To hear Him say, "Well done faithful servant,
Enter into the joy of the Lord."
Is the reason I keep pressing on,
It's the reason I live and die for.

Now, if you find yourself guilty of *exalting self* instead of *exalting Christ* in your ministry, there is hope! The fact that you are reading this book is a good indicator that you want to make sure Christ *is* the object of every performance, big or small, paid or unpaid. Knowing *the mission, connecting to the Master of the mission,* and *preparing for the mission* ensures that Christ will be center stage when you step up to the microphone to execute *the mission.*

To help you keep Christ center stage in your performances, I recommend do the following:

- Empty yourself of self. It will make room for the Holy Spirit.

- Keep a Christ-like attitude, especially when expectations fall short.

- Pray before, during, and after your performance that God's will be done.

- Be determined not to be a distraction nor be distracted by anyone or anything, including self.

- Incorporate scripture during your performance to link the message in the song to the Word and principles of God.

- Don't imply you are referring to God in your songs, but say His name, Jesus! There is life-changing power in that name and people need to hear it. Besides, isn't He what the ministry is all about?

- Last but not least, keep a humble and contrite spirit. For that is a spirit that the Holy Spirit can navigate and use.

As stated in our opening quote from E. G. White, *"Determine that (you) will have none of self but all of Jesus."* Furthermore, regarding your music ministry, let it not be said by our Savior, *"These people (Christian artists) come near me with their mouth and honor me with their lips (songs) but their hearts are far from me."* (Isaiah 29:13). Again, this is important to the mission because when we are on the stage, in the pulpit, or on whatever platform God provides, we are not showcasing our talent, but Jesus Christ, the Savior of the world. "If I be lifted up... I will draw all men unto me" (John 12:32). Be sure to lift Him up in your ministry.

MINISTRY CHECK

Keeping in mind that this is all about executing the mission, are you struggling with keeping Christ the center of attention in your performances? Before you open your mouth to speak or sing, do you first allow the Spirit to minister to you? Are you more concerned about what the audience has to say about your appearance and performance than what they have to say about Christ moving in their hearts as a result of your song and or spoken word ministry?

MINISTRY CHALLENGE

The next time you are scheduled to perform, take five minutes just before you are due on the stage; empty yourself of all non-ministry-related thoughts. Then pray and ask God to fill your mind with kingdom thoughts *(God's love, peace, joy, eternal life, redemption, etc.)* and recite John 12:32, *"And I, if I be lifted up from the earth, I will draw all men unto me"* so that you are sure to execute the mission His way. Then, later on, that evening, during your time of reflection *(we will discuss this in the next chapter)*, record your experience in a journal or on some other device. I promise you will be pleasantly surprised and blessed by your findings over time.

Reference Notes:

Ellen G. White, *Testimonies to Ministers and Gospel Workers,* 339

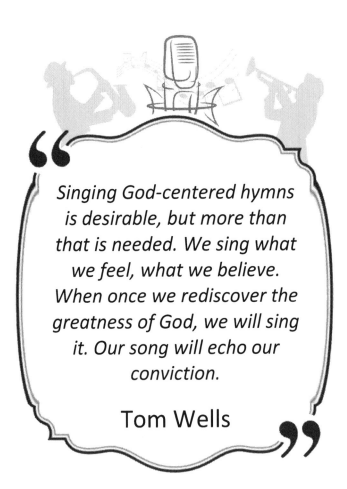

Singing God-centered hymns is desirable, but more than that is needed. We sing what we feel, what we believe. When once we rediscover the greatness of God, we will sing it. Our song will echo our conviction.

Tom Wells

CHAPTER 5

Executing the Mission (Part II):
Embrace the People

◆•◆•————————◆•◆◆•◆————————•◆•◆

We are called upon to love souls as Christ loved them.
(E. G. White)
Be kindly affectioned one to another with brotherly love.
(Romans 12:10)

While leaving the platform after singing one of my favorite songs, *Trust His Heart* by Babbie Mason, a young woman approached me and tearfully shared her joyous testimony of how God used me through that song to revive her hope and trust in God. She disclosed that she had a really challenging week where unfortunate things, beyond her control, happened to her that she felt were not deserved. It was a 'Job-like' experience, but unlike Job, she was not handling it well. She wanted to know why God was allowing the things to happen. In fact, she felt He had deserted her and wasn't hearing her prayers. But after hearing the lyrics to the chorus of the song, she was reminded that God had not forsaken her and that He is trustworthy and faithful to work all things for her good, no matter the situation. It gave her the hope and peace she needed to weather the storm.

Below are the lyrics to the chorus of the song, *Trust His Heart by Babbie Mason.* It has encouraged my heart over the years, and I pray it will do the same for you:

> *God is too wise to be mistaken,*
> *God is too good to be unkind.*
> *So when you don't understand,*
> *When you can't see His plan,*
> *When you can't trace His hand,*
> *Trust His Heart.*

What a beautiful testimony! I thank God for prompting the young woman to approach me and share her heart. But the above story could have had a not-so-happy ending if I wasn't Christ-centered.

What if I had sung my song and quickly exited the building or went to the green room to avoid speaking to anyone? Or what if she did approach me, but I was too tired or too eager to get to the product table to make some money that I brushed her off? Or what if my attitude was just *stank and stand-offish*, and she didn't feel comfortable sharing her heart with me? I guess the point I am getting at is this; if I didn't take the time to stop and speak with the woman, I would have missed an opportunity to be blessed by someone who I had just ministered to in addition to missing out on the blessing God was sending me via her testimony.

As I mentioned earlier in the book, it is a benefit to me when others share how my obedience to God in ministry blessed them. It affirms what I am called to do. This affirmation keeps me going during the low periods of my life when the enemy is working fervently and ferociously to take me down. It keeps me grounded in God and not in myself. But, it doesn't stop there.

When an artist chooses to avoid the people they minister to, they also deprive people of an opportunity to experience the joy of sharing their heart and testimony with the person who was the catalyst of it—the artist. As a Believer, you know to what joy I am referring. It's that joy you experience when you discover something new and wonderful that will make your life better, such as a new born baby, a job promotion, or in this case, the ultimate joy that comes from knowing a loving and trustworthy God.

I don't know about you, but I don't want that ever to be the case regarding my ministry. I want people to see, hear and feel Christ before, during and after I minister. It is part of my mission to physically touch people, when possible, so that they receive the benefits of a Spirit-filled touch. Personally speaking, I am truly blessed when a Christian brother or sister, filled with the Holy Spirit, reaches out to physically embrace me. It can be very encouraging, soothing, and even healing, depending on what is going on in my life at that time.

So when we, as artists, physically embrace someone via a handshake, hug, and or holy kiss, we are ministering just as much at that moment, as we are when we are on stage. It is what Christ did, and He has instructed us to do the same (see 1 Thessalonians 5:6; 2 Corinthians 13:12).

I don't just physically embrace people. I also continue to touch people with my words when talking with them face-to-face. I make it my purpose to listen attentively, prayerfully, and empathically. I don't want to miss an opportunity for the Lord to use me at that moment.

As I write the conclusion of this chapter, it is my prayer that you make it your priority to deliver a Spirit-led performance on and off stage by embracing the people both verbally and physically. I deeply believe that what we do before and after the performance is just as important as what we do during the performance.

I believe, whole-heartedly, it is imperative that people feel that you genuinely care about them. And I can't think of a better way to relay that message than to physically embrace them when given the opportunity. A gentle touch goes a long way, and a *Spirit-filled* touch goes even further.

Remember, part of the mission is that people see and hear Christ in us always—on and off the stage.

MINISTRY CHECK

How about you?   As a Christian artist, when you have completed your performance, what is your mindset at the time? Do you rush to get to the greenroom, product table, or car with the intent to avoid personal contact with people? Do you lack empathy and Christian love for the souls who sat listening to you sing and speak about the love of God? Furthermore, what will people have to say about your representation of Christ when they encounter you up close and personal? Will they see an extension of the Christ you just sang and spoke about, or will they sum you up as just another Godless performer?

MINISTRY CHALLENGE

If your answer is yes or you are uncertain about the answers to any of the above questions, I earnestly challenge you to take some time to pray and seek God. Seek His wisdom for why you feel this way towards His children—your brothers and sisters—as well as the what must you do, surrender, and or confess that you might receive a changed heart—a Christ-like heart.

Also, try to remember a time when you were going through a rough period in your life, and someone with Godly love embraced you? How did it make you feel? Write it down in your journal as a reminder and guide for you as you minister to others.

Below are lyrics from the song *When the Music Stops* by gospel artist and songwriter Daryl Coley. As you read through them, honestly and prayerfully ask yourself if the lyrics are true for you. If the answer is no, ask God to forgive you for living a lie, to help you to live according to the truth, and then help you recommit your life to executing the mission *His* way.

Reference Notes:

Ellen G. White, *Evangelism*,
https://text.egwwritings.org/publicationtoc.php?bookCode
=Ev&lang=en&collection=2&section=all .

When the Music Stops
Daryl Coley

When the music stops,
That's when I live my song
When the band goes home,
That's when I live my song
When we've said Amen,
And the crowd begins to fade away
That's when I live the life,
That I sing about in my song
If I sing a song of love,
I've got to live it
If I sing a song of joy,
I've got to live it
If I sing a song of peace,
If I sing a song of happiness,
I've got to live the life,
that I sing about in my song

> "*Soloists should remember that they are rendering the highest service when called on to sing or play. Only one's very best should be brought to the service of God...no mediocre musician should be permitted to play merely because of his consecration, for this would not represent the high standard of God's work.*
>
> Marrison A. Offer"

CHAPTER 6

Maintaining the Mission

And after He had dismissed the multitudes,
He went up into the hills by Himself to pray.
(Matthew 14:23)

I don't know about you, but when I finish ministering, whether it is in song or spoken word, I feel as though my soul has been emptied and left feeling physically weak and worn. What this tells me is that it is time for replenishment and renewal of both my body and soul. But this is nothing new to those in ministry, including Jesus and his disciples. Look at what Matthew 6:30-32 (Amplified) states:

30 The apostles [sent out as missionaries] came back and gathered together to Jesus, and told Him all that they had done and taught.

31 And He said to them, [As for you] come away by yourselves to a deserted place, and rest a while—for many were [continually] coming and going, and they had not even leisure enough to eat.

32 And they went away in a boat to a solitary place by themselves.

Even Jesus knew the importance of getting away after ministering to the people to replenish, both physically and spiritually.

It doesn't take a genius to know that you cannot get something from nothing. And in order to sustain your ministry and mission, you must routinely refresh your spiritual and physical being after ministry, just as Jesus did.

I like how *John Gill's Exposition of the Whole Bible*, interprets Mark 6:31:

And he said unto them: *After he had heard their account, was satisfied with it, and approved of what they had said and done:*

come ye yourselves apart into a desert place, and rest a while: *where they might be free from noise and hurry, and take some rest and refreshment, after their wearisome journey, hard labors, and great fatigue in preaching and working miracles; which shows the great compassion, tenderness, and care of Christ, for his disciples:*

for there were many coming and going, and they had no leisure so much as to eat; *the people were continually going to and fro; as soon as one company was gone, who came with their sick and diseased to be healed, or upon one account or another, another came: so that there was no opportunity of private meditation and prayer, nor of spiritual converse together: nor even so much as to eat a meal's meat for the refreshment of nature.*

Here, we can see Jesus' love and concern for His disciples' well-being. He instructed them to come away from the crowds and their duties to rest and refresh themselves.

As followers of Christ, wanting to maintain our commitment to the mission, we must not allow ourselves to become spiritually and physically vulnerable to the enemy by neglecting to replenish our body *(with healthy foods and rest)* and spirit *(with spiritual food—prayer and the Word of God).* We must determine to be spiritually and physically alert so as not to be deceived or distracted by the frivolous and destructive ways of the world while we labor to reach souls for Christ.

In case you didn't know, taking time to rest and recover is a common practice among athletes who, after a competitive match or even after days of intense training, rest from strenuous physical activity. They know that if they don't take a break, their body will do it for them at an inopportune time. With that said, being that we too are spiritual athletes running a long-distance race, we need to pace ourselves and follow the example of Christ and the apostles to ensure we not only finish the race but that we finish it strong.

To ensure that I consistently replenish physically and spiritually during the mission, I take off the Monday following a weekend of ministry. Monday is my carefree day to take care of me. So if I don't want to talk to anyone outside of my family, I don't. If I don't feel like exercising or cleaning the house, I don't. If I don't want to get out of bed until midday, I don't. You get my point. When I incorporate Bible reading, meditation and prayer, and songs of praise, I find this sabbatical very refreshing and invigorating to my spirit, mind, and body.

A misconception some Christian artists have is that their ministry is for others and not for themselves. That couldn't be farther from the truth! When you are on stage, sharing and delivering the message of Jesus Christ to others, you are ministering to yourself as well. The message in the music is just as much for you as it is for them. You, as the artist, must lead by example, and that can only happen if you have an intimate and genuine relationship with Christ. How else can you convince others to have a relationship with Him?

But to go a step further, when the music stops, the people go home, and you are left alone; your time of spiritual reflection should begin. Spending quality time with God, post-ministry, is an excellent way for you to listen for what He has to say to you. In other words, this time allows you to grow spiritually and to grow in grace.

Here is another way to look at your time of replenishment. During your performance, you are ministering to the people. But during your time of renewal, God is ministering to you. And He knows exactly what you need. Isn't that awesome!

During our refreshment period with God, we can unload and give the cares and concerns people have shared with us, as well as our own. It is an opportunity to intercede on their behalf and ask for God's blessing and favor upon them and ourselves. During our refreshment period, we are able to unload and give the cares and concerns people have shared with us, as well as our own, to God. We are able to intercede on their behalf and ask for God's blessing and favor upon them and ourselves.

You may be thinking that your ministry is not as intense as the disciples' or Jesus' ministry; therefore, you don't need to replenish after each performance. But I tell you, whether you are in full-time or part-time ministry, you need to take time after each performance to reflect and refresh your body and spirit.

What I am about to share with you is very personal, but I am sharing it as a warning to you as a fellow artist in ministry. If you're not grounded in Christ, the enemy and your flesh will rise against and in you with a vengeance, and you will fall prey to them.

For well over 30 years, I have been singing at some level of ministry. During the performances when the Holy Spirit was heavy upon me and the audience, the following day or so, I'd find myself struggling with the spirit of depression. I couldn't explain it at the time. All I knew was that I was feeling worthless and spiritually weak.

Well, one day, while I was going through one of these episodes, a close friend and sister-in-Christ called me and told me that I was under attack by the enemy. She went on to say that she noticed the pattern I had developed of pulling away from her and refusing to talk soon after I had finished ministering. I couldn't deny it. It was true, but I didn't know how to fix it, or so I thought.

On the one hand, I needed to pull away from people after a period of intense ministry, while on the other hand, I needed to use that time to replenish my soul. But, I wasn't being replenished, at least not adequately. I was recharging physically but not spiritually. Instead of reflecting on what God and I had accomplished through ministry, I was filled with despair from thoughts of worthlessness and negative thinking. Physically fatigued and spiritually drained, I would let depression get the best of me. I would even take it a step further to question God's call on my life. Then, I would feel ashamed for feeling this way and couldn't pray. It was a vicious cycle. How quickly after singing His praises, I forgot about His amazing grace, love, and mercy towards me, giving the enemy a foothold in my life.

In hindsight, I now know how this reoccurring cycle persisted. Instead of focusing on the state of my flesh— flesh that is condemned to death—I should have been in prayer and meditation with the Father. And when I read Galatians 2:20, that says, *"I have been crucified with Christ; it's no longer I who live, but Christ who lives in me; and the life which I **now** live in the flesh, I live by faith in the Son of God, who loved me and gave Himself for me.",* I would have been reminded that the Devil is a liar, and the truth is not in him! That I was bought with the priceless blood of Jesus Christ, and covered with His robe of righteousness; thus, no need to feel condemned and ashamed.

But it doesn't stop there!

God goes on to assure me in John 14:6 that *"(He) is the Way, Truth, and Life."* As long as I am His, I have eternal life and no one can take it away from me, except me, if I decide to believe the lies of the enemy. And by God's grace, I won't!

So here is my point. Once I gave the spirit of depression over to God, He gave me His Spirit of Peace that He promises in Isaiah 26:3, *"Thou wilt keep him in perfect peace, whose mind is stayed on thee: because he trusteth in thee."* What that scripture tells me is that if I keep Christ-centered in my life, my mind will always be on Him. As a result, I experience perfect peace within so that there is no room for depression, negative thoughts, and the lies of Satan. In other words, the Devil has no dominion over me! Now that is something to sing and shout about! *Hallelujah and Amen!*

So if you find yourself under the attack of the enemy because of your ministry, just know that God is able and willing to deliver and keep you as long as you keep your mind on Him. In doing so, you will be able to maintain your commitment to God and His mission.

So to recap, maintaining your commitment to the mission is to:

- fortify and replenish your spirit daily, especially right before and after ministering, by spending quality time in Bible reading and prayer.

- get the proper rest and nutrients for your body.

- cast all of the cares of the people you meet upon Christ. Remember, you are not their Savior but the messenger.

- give God the praise and thanks continuously; for when the heart is thankful, and the lips are expressing appreciation, there is no room for doubt, fear, and defeat.

- last but not least, keep Christ center stage in every performance by having at the forefront of your mind and the top of your priority list the mission— sharing the Good News of Jesus Christ.

MINISTRY CHECK:

What do you do to maintain your commitment to the mission? Is it working for you or do you need to revisit and revamp your maintenance plan?

MINISTRY CHALLENGE:

Write out a commitment statement to God detailing what you will do to maintain your commitment to God's mission—sharing the Gospel of Jesus Christ on and off stage. Remember to include building on your relationship with Christ and taking care of your body and mind—the fundamental elements for sustaining a Christ-centered ministry.

Once you have completed the statement, type it, frame it, and place it somewhere you can see it easily as a daily reminder of your commitment to the mission.

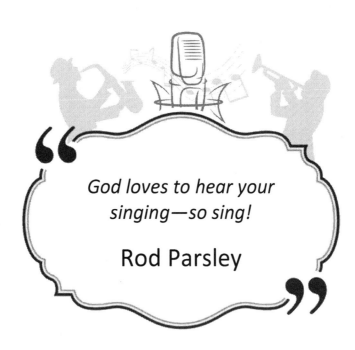

God loves to hear your
singing—so sing!

Rod Parsley

CHAPTER 7

Mission Accomplished

Blessed (happy, to be envied) is the man who is patient under trial and stands up under temptation, for when he has stood the test and been approved, he will receive [the victor's] crown of life which God has promised to those who love Him. (James 1:12, AMP)

By now, I'd like to think that the previous chapters have captivated your attention, piqued your interest, and motivated you to take a closer look at your music ministry. More importantly, I hope you have determined to make and keep Christ centered in your life, and the focus of your message, whether you are singing a song or sharing a spoken word, anything less would not be ministry.

As believers, whether a singer or not, we have a responsibility to know and share the Gospel of Jesus Christ with nonbelievers so that they might be saved (Mark 16:15-16). Additionally, we are to love, forgive, and encourage each other as brothers and sisters in the Lord, serving each other with humility and grace (I Peters 3:8). It is the commission that Christ gave His disciples, and this is still the mission for Believers today.

As a Christian artist, I know the pressure and enticement of the music industry personally, even in the gospel sect. The desire to be 'successful', according to industry standards, plagues Christian artists worldwide. In the music industry, success for an artist happens when they sell at least 100,000 CDs (gold status), are nominated for an industry award (Billboard, BET, Grammy), and have all of the luxuries (expensive house, cars, apparel and jewelry) that come with the lifestyle of a celebrity. In other words, you are successful when you are *living large!*

Being transparent at this moment, I will admit that my attitude about my music ministry has been less than godly. There were times when I didn't and wouldn't take engagements that didn't meet specific criteria such as a particular platform and honorarium amount. After all, I had bills to pay and a preferred lifestyle to maintain.

And if that weren't bad enough, I would wait until the very last minute to select songs and practice them on the way to the event. And don't let me only sell a handful of CDs! It was during these times I thought, *Who are they to waste my time and energy singing on a poorly planned and supported program? Don't they know God called me to do this for a living, and they have a responsibility in making sure I am a success?*

Crazy, right? But that is where I was at different periods of my ministry journey. That is where I was when *I* took center stage instead of Christ. I had gotten Matthew 6:33 backward and totally twisted! Instead of seeking God first, I was seeking *stuff* and *status.*

Now, I am not saying that there is anything wrong with having financial success in your music ministry. I hope to, God willing. But, as a Christian artist—a disciple of Christ—you must be careful how *you* define success as it relates to your faith.

So let's define success.

According to dictionary.com, success is *"the attainment of wealth, position, honors, and the like; the accomplishment of one's goal."* Sound familiar? Of course it does. It sounds like the music industry's definition. But let's look at what *real* success is as a Christian artist.

In my opinion, *"the accomplishment of one's goal,"* is where the definition of 'success' for a Christian should begin and end. As a follower of Christ, my mission and goal is to share the Gospel of Jesus Christ, not to collect earthly accolades and material things. To say anything different would not be biblical. I would go further to add that there is nothing in the Bible that says if someone is in the ministry, they will or should be wealthy, famous, or honored. In fact, it states the opposite. The Apostle Paul makes it crystal clear that the work in ministry is neither glamorous nor financially rewarding. But don't take my word for it; read it for yourself:

> *10 We are [looked upon as] fools on account of Christ and for His sake, but you are [supposedly] so amazingly wise and prudent in Christ! We are weak, but you are [so very] strong! You are highly esteemed, but we are in disrepute and contempt! 11 To this hour we have*

gone both hungry and thirsty; we [habitually] wear but one undergarment [and shiver in the cold]; we are roughly knocked about and wander around homeless. 12 And we still toil unto weariness [for our living], working hard with our own hands. When men revile us [wound us with an accursed sting], we bless them. When we are persecuted, we take it patiently and endure it. 13 When we are slandered and defamed, we [try to] answer softly and bring comfort. We have been made and are now the rubbish and filth of the world [the off scouring of all things, the scum of the earth]. 14 I do not write this to shame you, but to warn and counsel you as my beloved children. 15 After all, though you should have ten thousand teachers (guides to direct you) in Christ, yet you do not have many fathers. For I became your father in Christ Jesus through the glad tidings (the Gospel). 16 So I urge and implore you, be imitators of me. 17 For this very cause I sent to you Timothy, who is my beloved and trustworthy child in the Lord, who will recall to your minds my methods of proceeding and course of conduct and way of life in Christ, such as I teach everywhere in each of the churches. I Corinthians 4:10 -17 (AMP)

There you have it! The apostles were not wealthy men with bottomless bank accounts; nor, in some cases, were they homeowners. The ministry was funded by the faith and generosity and support of the church members. And when that wasn't enough, the apostles worked to make up the deficit.

With the awareness of the above-mentioned Bible texts, it puzzles me that Christian artists (like myself at one time) equate financial wealth and accolades to ministry success when it is biblically clear that wealth and fame are not promised benefits or outcomes of a Christ-centered ministry.

Again, to be clear, I am NOT saying that it is a bad thing to obtain wealth as a result of your ministry (especially when it is grounded in God), but don't let wealth and accolades be the *goal* of your ministry. Remember, our ultimate goal is to share the good news of Jesus Christ and His unfailing love for humanity. And if we do not experience wealth and fame in our ministry, let us not lose sight of the task at hand, which is to complete the mission Christ has given us. Be confident of this thing; when Christ returns to gather His faithful children unto Himself, then we will receive the greatest, reward ever—the gift of eternal life! And let's not forget the mortgage-free mansion, the golden, starry crown, the long white robe and the streets of gold! *Cha Ch'ing!* Now that's living large!

With that said, I am very thankful that God checked me when I got caught up in myself. It is only by His grace I am pursuing His will for my music ministry. And after He reminded me of what the ministry mission was, is and will continue to be, I honestly can say I wouldn't have it any other way.

So, if I never receive a man-made Dove, Stellar, or Grammy award, it's all right with me. As long as I complete my Father's mission, I am a success—an *eternal* success!

In closing, I'd like to share one of my favorite hymns, *I'd Rather Have Jesus.* I had the privilege of recording it has a part of a medley on my debut CD, *From You.* The author, Rhea F. Miller, couldn't have penned it better; for it states that there is nothing in this world (no matter how great its value) worth losing your soul for. I second that, and I'll even inject this. There is nothing more important to keep me from completing my divine mission. If you agree with me, recite or sing the lyrics below out loud as you recommit yourself entirely to the mission God has given you.

I Rather Have Jesus

Verse:

I rather have Jesus, than silver or gold.

I rather be His, than have riches untold.

I rather have Jesus, than houses or land.

I rather be led by His nail pierced hands.

Chorus:

Then to be a King (Queen) of a vast domain,

Or be held in sin's dread sway.

I rather have Jesus, than anything,

This old world affords today.

Verse:

I'd rather have Jesus than men's applause;

I'd rather be faithful to His dear cause;

I'd rather have Jesus than worldwide fame;

I'd rather be true to His holy name

MINISTRY CHECK

What about you? Would you rather have Jesus overworld fame and fortune with your ministry? Are you determined to complete the mission at all costs? Or have you sold out the Gospel of Jesus Christ for the temporal and despicable things of this world?

Time is both too short and precious to waste on things that won't matter when it comes down to the end. God has entrusted you with a powerful, influential instrument and gift; when you dedicate it to His use and cause, it can help you reach lost and discouraged souls for Him.

MINISTRY CHALLENGE

If up until now, you have been struggling with your music ministry—keeping it Christ centered, wanting the accolades of people more than the accolades of God—and now you are convicted by the Holy Spirit that things need to change, I challenge you to start today. Right now! Start fresh by vowing you are *"forgetting those things which are behind* (letting go of past mistakes and poor choices regarding your life and ministry), *and reaching forth unto those things which are before* (boldly and confidently looking to the future God has for you and your ministry), *I press toward the mark for the prize of the high calling of God in Christ Jesus* (you are determined that nothing will come before or between you and God and His gift of eternal life)." *(Philippians 3:13 - 14)*

To help you in the process, review highlights from this book:

- <u>Commit to the Divine Mission</u>
  Share the Gospel of Jesus Christ. (Matt. 28:19)

- <u>Get and Stay Connected to God</u>
  The Master of the Mission. (Phil. 4:13)

- <u>Determine to Do All Things Well in Your Ministry</u>
  God expects it. (Eccl. 9:10a)

- <u>Keep Christ at the Center of Your Performance</u>
  Only God should be exalted. (John 12:32)

- <u>Embrace Mankind</u>
  Like Christ, love and serve them. (Phil. 2:1- 4,23)

- <u>Take Time to Replenish</u>
  You can't give from nothing. (Mark 6:30 - 32)

- <u>Don't Compromise the Mission and Lose Your</u>
  <u>Soul</u>—It's not worth it. (Mark 8:36)

So when the temptations of the world (including those of the gospel music industry) begin to weigh heavily upon you, and you are tempted to compromise your ministry and mission for the riches of this world, remember your vow and the question found in Mark 8:36, NLT. *"And what do you benefit if you gain the whole world but lose your own soul?"* Then, determine to let nothing or no one come between you and your Savior. And let nothing and no one hinder you from accomplishing the mission God has given you.

My final challenge to you as a Christian artist is to keep your ministry in check by ***Keeping Christ Center Stage!***

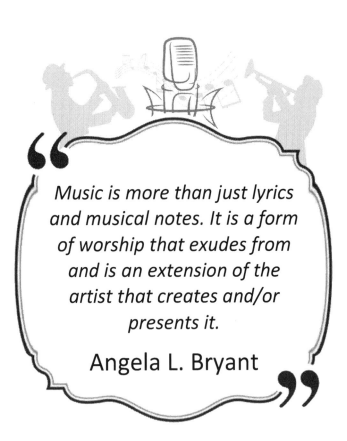

Music is more than just lyrics and musical notes. It is a form of worship that exudes from and is an extension of the artist that creates and/or presents it.

Angela L. Bryant

CHAPTER 8

Handling Your Business

◆·◆·············◆·◆·◆·◆·◆················◆·◆

In the same way, the Lord has commanded that those who preach the Gospel should receive their living from the Gospel. (I Corinthians 9:14)

In my 25 plus years of music ministry, the topic of whether Christian artists should be compensated for their ministry has been debated. As a result, artists like myself have struggled with how to address compensation when booking ourselves at various churches and their related events. And although I am addressing this topic towards the end of this book, it is not to be perceived as least important.

Commonly asked questions like, "Should a person in ministry be compensated? And if yes, how much? " is discussed in Christian organizations worldwide, despite what **Proverbs 3:27** says, *Do not withhold good from those to whom it is due, when it is in your power to do it.* Therefore, I would be doing a disservice to my readers to not speak to this topic. So I shall!

Regardless of what people and organizations think, it is the responsibility of the artist to decide whether or not they want to get compensated for their contribution to the ministry. After all, organizations are *not buying* what you offer in ministry, but rather, they are *affording* you to continue to work in ministry at a level of excellence God expects and requires, and so should they.

In the following paragraphs, I will share with you why it is perfectly okay to require an honorarium and what to consider when determining the amount, as well as briefly discuss the importance of using a contract to secure ministry dates.

> **Disclaimer:** *The information and personal opinions stated in this chapter are not necessarily for all musicians. It is primarily for those musicians who are called to full-*

> *time ministry, meaning that the majority, if not all, of their*
> *livelihood comes from the ministry.*

Biblical Examples of People in Ministry Being Compensated

Since the establishment of the earthly temple of God, there have been both full-time Levitical priests and musicians attending to the services and upkeep of the temple. That means that they were not allowed to work another job. It was forbidden because they were called to serve God in this capacity. So how were their daily provisions provided? Who fed, clothed, and sheltered them and their families? The Israelites!

What I love about God—Jehovah Jireh, our provider—Is that He leaves nothing for man to guess when it comes to taking care of *The Mission,* which is to evangelize the world. He even gave us a model in the Bible on how to compensate the temple workers, which include the Levitical priests and musicians. And it is so simple. They are to be taken care of with the offerings and tithes of the people for their lifetime dedication to the church.

If you wonder what was and still is the criteria for the ministry leaders and musicians, the Bible says that these workers were highly skilled, trained, and gifted in their services and were engrossed in their work, day and night.

What this says to me is that musicians who have, 1) identified their gift and call to the ministry and 2) committed to the highest development of it, so much that they cannot possibly hold another position or occupation without compromising the ministry, *should* be compensated. How else would they provide for their basic needs? And let's face it. No one wants to needlessly exhaust their time and energy, holding down multiple jobs trying to make ends meet if the option to hold one fairly compensated position is possible. Life is too short to waste on tasks that hold lesser value, and James 4:14b, ESV, couldn't have made this point more crystal clear: "What is your life? For you are a mist that appears for a little time and then vanishes." Amen!

For those readers who are still not convinced that it is biblical for musicians to receive compensation for their service, the following bible texts are for your consideration:

- **I Chronicles 9:33 (NASB)** states, "Now these are the singers, heads of fathers' households of the

Levites, who lived in the chambers of the temple free from other service; for they were engaged in their work day and night."

- **I Chronicles 25:6-7 (NASB)** states, "All these (singers) were under the direction of their father to sing in the house of the LORD, with cymbals, harps and lyres, for the service of the house of God... Their number who were trained in singing to the LORD, with their relatives, all who were skillful..."

- **Deuteronomy 18:1-5 (ESV)** states, "The Levitical priests, all the tribe of Levi, shall have no portion or inheritance with Israel. They shall eat the LORD's food offerings as their inheritance. [2] They shall have no inheritance among their brothers; the LORD is their inheritance, as he promised them. [3] And this shall be the priests' due from the people, from those offering a sacrifice, whether an ox or a sheep: they shall give to the priest the shoulder and the two cheeks and the stomach. [4] The first fruits of your grain, of your wine and of your oil, and the first fleece of your sheep, you shall give him. [5] For the LORD your God has chosen him out of all your tribes to stand and minister in the name of the LORD, him and his sons for all time.

But if the Old Testament isn't sufficient, look at what the New Testament has to say:

- **Luke 10:7 (ESV)**: "And remain in the same house, eating and drinking what they provide, for the laborer deserves his wages..."

- **Matthew 10:8:** "Freely ye have received, freely give."

- **Matt. 10:10:** "The workman is worthy of his meat." Full-time or part-time, work is work.

Some could try to argue that the above-stated texts support the view that those in ministry should be open to whatever the church they are ministering at has to offer and not set or request an honorarium. In other words, musicians should expect love offerings versus set honorariums. And I would somewhat agree with them if the home church of these full-time musicians were providing for their families as outlined and previously done in the Old and New Testament temple and churches. But it is clearly not that way today. Therefore, musicians have the right and obligation to determine what they need to provide for themselves and their families. Compensation is commonly in the form of a set honorarium or a love offering. In some cases, if the church has a small congregation, a combination of both is used. In addition to compensation, most full-time artists and musicians have invested in recording music CDs, DVDs, books, and other paraphernalia for purchase to help fund and expand their ministry, as well as enhance the worship experience of the Believer on a daily basis. Now let's land on this topic. It is well within the biblical rights of an artist or musician to require compensation for their services. After all, if their ministry is centered in Christ, they are spreading the Gospel. And as stated above in our opening text (I Corinthians 9:14), "Those who preach (or sing) the Gospel should receive their living from the Gospel."

Enough said...let's move on!

Determining an Honorarium

Defining Honorarium:

- a fee for services rendered by a professional person (Freedictionary.com)

- an amount of money paid for a service (Merriam-Webster)

As previously discussed, "The workman is worthy of his meat." (Matt. 10: 10.) The obvious questions to answer are, "Is my ministry (service) worthy of compensation? And how does that translate into monetary value?

Let me first say that what I am going to suggest is not etched in stone, penned in ink, or a one-size-fit-all answer or formula. Rather, it is my personal process for setting an honest and fair honorarium. So, please, feel free to take all, some, or none of it for your use.

Second, in response to the question, "Is my ministry (service) worthy of compensation?," Based on the previously mentioned bible texts, the answer is YES, ABSOLUTELY, and SHO NUF (slang for "sure enough". LOL!)! But here is one more text just in case you still need a little more convincing. First Timothy 5:18 restates what the scriptures say in both the old and new testaments, "For the Scripture says, 'Do not muzzle an ox while it is treading out the grain,' (Duet 25:4) and 'The worker deserves his wages.'" (Luke 10:7).

End of discussion!

Last but not least, let's look at how I set a monetary value to my ministry, should you choose to do the same.

When I first started in full-time ministry, I had no clue what to charge or ask for in a market that is still debating whether or not a Christian musician should be compensated for their service—I wish someone had written a book like this back then (SMH). With a narrow perspective in the minds of most church leaders and members, it was quite a challenge setting monetary amounts without turning them off or offending them. In some cases, I found it to be unnerving and disheartening when negotiating honorarium with Christian organizations. To this day, it amazes me that musicians are expected to *play* like professionals but not receive the *pay* of a professional. It is safe to say that no one in a chosen occupation reports to work (full or part-time) and not expect to receive compensation for his or her contribution to the organization. That would be ludicrous and illegal, even.

So why are the demands different for Christian artists and musicians? Only heaven knows!

After several years in ministry, I find the following practices to be very helpful in setting honorarium and fee amounts:

1. **Pray for guidance** –James 1:5 says that "If any of you lack wisdom, let him (her) ask of God, that giveth to all men liberally." In other words, when in doubt ask God for guidance. In my experience, He has helped me to discern when to accept or decline an invitation to minister as well as what to ask for in honorarium. And He will do the same for you. He is no respecter of persons (see Acts 10:34).

2. **Know the industry norm in your market(s)** –It is always wise to research what your peers are charging in your industry, precisely what's the standard honorarium in your local and regional markets to assess and determine a fair starting point. But while doing so, be careful to compare your level of experience with those similar to it. To say it another way, compare apples with apples and oranges with oranges. For example, when I first started in 2005 in the DC metro area, the average honorarium or suggested love offering for

unsigned artists was anywhere from $75 - 150 per song and $300 - 600 for a 45 - 60-minute concert, depending on your level of market recognition or how well you negotiated. In most, if not all cases, travel-related expenses or live musicians were an additional cost. Therefore, I set my minimum honorarium at $75 per song plus mileage back then. Once I gained more experience and exposure via television and live performances. After factoring in the cost of living increase (*yes, I did.*), I increased my honorarium each year while remaining within my market's norm. Take away point? Do your research, so you don't shortchange yourself or overcharge your clients.

3. **Know your budget** –There is nothing worse than getting to the end of a month and realize you do not have enough *Benjamins, Jacksons,* or *Washingtons* to cover your expenses. To reduce the risk of coming up short financially each month, set a realistic monthly budget according to what you need (tithe & offering, living, medical, and dental expenses, taxes, etc.) and even include some of what you want (vacations, hobbies, social outings,

etc.) within reason. And please don't forget to put something into your savings! Once you have the budget in place, then you can wisely set your honorarium (including a sliding scale) while ensuring you are not shortchanging yourself and the quality of your ministry.

4. **Be flexible** –Over the years, I have found the use of a sliding fee scale very beneficial being that it affords for more organizations, especially nonprofits whose pockets vary in depth, to take advantage of my services. What you don't want to happen is for you to be frequently overlooked because you refuse to be flexible with your fee. Remember, it is ministry first and money second. Besides, if other secular organizations can offer a sliding fee scale so that as many people as possible can take advantage of what they have to offer, then those of us in ministry should feel compelled to follow suit. After all, we are offering something both invaluable and eternal that is destined to change people's lives for the *best*. With that said, I strongly suggest and encourage you to avoid turning down ministry requests and opportunities

when at all possible. Remember to pray before you turn away☺.

5. **Be Confident** –When stating your honorarium, be confident knowing that what you are asking for is fair and justified. The quickest way to kill your chances of receiving your requested honorarium is to sound uncertain or timid when stating it to the client. It gives the impression that you are not comfortable with your ask and thus not worth your fee. So be confident!

6. **Recruit Help** – If you find negotiating your honorarium and other ministry-related terms and conditions to be unnerving, ask someone you not only trust but also is competent in this area to handle it for you. You may have to pay a small service fee (if not done out of the goodness of their heart), but it will be well worth it.

Writing the Contract: It's the professional thing to do.

I find it ironic that some church leaders have a problem with artists using contracts when God has used contracts (covenants) since the beginning of time. According to

Merriam-Webster dictionary, a *covenant* is "a written agreement or promise usually under seal between two or more parties especially for the performance of some action," and a *contract* is "a legal agreement between people, companies, etc." So they are one and the same. Yet it's still a problem many artists deal with today.

In my 25 plus years in ministry, I have experienced severe pushback when submitting a contract to church leaders. They don't understand why I need to get it in writing. "After all, we are Christians and should trust each other.", they say. But anyone with half a brain knows that when a service is rendered in exchange for a fee or honorarium, they better get it in writing (if they know what's good for them) or take the risk of being cheated or shortchanged. It applies to *ALL* organizations because all organizations are made up of imperfect people with good and bad intentions. And in case you didn't know already, good intentions do not pay bills.

Moving right along, I'd like to say that in my many years of service that I have been treated fairly by most churches that have invited me to minister before their congregation, but I would be telling a lie. Too often, I've received a fraction of my honorarium while still expected to come in a day earlier or leave out a day later so that they can get a cheaper flight, totally disregarding the unwarranted and wasted time away from my family and other obligations.

So, when I strongly suggest, and even insist, that you use a contract when booking engagements, I am speaking from personal experience. Without a contract in place, you will find yourself being taken advantage of by both church and secular organizations.

I recall one particular time when I sent over a contract for an international engagement and had a difficult time getting the contract signed after they agreed to the terms. Weeks and months had gone by, and I still hadn't received the signed contract. It was three weeks before I was due to fly out, and I had not yet applied for my visa because I wanted to, at minimum, receive the signed contract committing both parties to the agreement BEFORE spending the money for it.

Finally, I received the signed contract two weeks prior to my departure date after sending a final email stating that I would be forced to decline their invitation unless I received the signed contract or flight confirmation within

48 hours. But as a result of their delay in getting me the agreement, the organization was unable to purchase my airline ticket due to its astronomical price, forcing them to cancel the concert.

Now, if I hadn't received a signed contract before they canceled the concert, I would have lost the expected revenue from that engagement. But as a result of having a signed contract in place, they had to pay me 50% of my honorarium, as stated in the agreement, for canceling less than two weeks before the event. And it was a good thing too because I had turned down another engagement for that same weekend.

I share this with you to emphasize the importance of using a contract, even in ministry, especially if it is your livelihood—partial or whole. Another way to look at it is, as Christians, it is our duty to be honorable with our word and to hold each other accountable. That is what having a contract in place does.

Drafting a contract doesn't have to be a lengthy and challenging process. There are many free templates and samples on the world wide web if you don't know where to start. I drew up my own contract and rider (will explain a little later) that is no more than two pages long. I keep it very simple because most of my engagements are with churches that have the standard setup—church podium as the stage, an in-house PA system (in most cases) and floor monitors. Keeping the contract short but thorough in detail helps reduce or eliminate the overwhelming feeling church leaders sometime experience when dealing with artists and musicians. So again, if at all possible, keep it short.

Depending on the size of your band, when drafting a contract, you may also need to include a separate rider to include technical (i.e., sound, lighting) and professional (i.e., meals, travel details) requirements for all of your team members. I say, "may need to" because I didn't use one when I first started. Since I was a solo act for the most part, I incorporated my technical and professional requirements within my 1-2-page contract. As I previously mentioned, most churches are similar in setup, so I knew what they typically had or didn't have and stated in the contract/tech rider the required items that were needed so that they knew in advance and could provide them. In other words, I wanted to make sure my live performance and their audience's experience was exceptional by

KEEPING CHRIST CENTER STAGE

making sure we were all on the same page via a written contract. Still, I kept the contract simple in order to reduce the chance of overwhelming the client; and I still do to this day.

In cases where I am performing at a large venue outside of a typical church setting, I do have a rider—again, a document used to outline the technical and personal requirements of the artist—that is an addendum to my contract. These performances usually happen with large and lucrative organizations where money is not an issue. In this case, I would probably bring a 4-piece band and three background singers. Therefore, I need to be more detailed when stating what I need avoid unnecessary hiccups and to assure a great performance. Also, it is the norm to request green rooms for the band members along with private accommodations. I like to call these accommodations "perks" because they are not mandatory (unless dealing with a Diva or Divo) but rather a hospitable gesture by the host. For instance, one organization honored my request in my rider to have a fruit basket and herbal tea with honey in my green room. Again, it was not a requirement but a request that the host honored. And I was very grateful☺.

On a side note, I must talk about some of the ridiculous contract riders I have heard about and seen. There are riders that are 15 pages long, spelling out not only the technical needs, but the artist's wants, wishes, and anything else that tickles their fancy. I don't mean to sound cynical, but as Christian artists, we need to do better. Just because the industry says it is the norm to list everything under the sun in your rider doesn't mean we should. Organizations such as the church, who are in many cases operating on a tight budget, would better use their funds on the essentials that directly impact ministry versus spending money accommodating artists' petty requests. The following are outrageous demands artists have requested in their rider:

- That the venue install a brand-new toilet seat in the dressing room bathroom before they arrive.

- That the venue provide a 40-foot trailer furnished all in white from top to bottom—flowers, tablecloths, drapery, couches, candles, and so on.

- That a dressing room is filled with buckets of spicy fried chicken, lemonade, and only candles that smell of baked goods.

- That the driver is forbidden to make eye contact with or speak to them.

- That the lodging provisions include a 1-bedroom presidential suite at a 5 star hotel, free internet service, and complimentary breakfast for the entire touring party—drivers, singers, band members, engineer.

Of course, not every artist practices this kind of behavior. But the point I want to get across is that as a Christian artist, we need to keep demands and requests in our contract and rider simple. None of the above requirements has anything to do with their performance. These are just self-centered demands feeding their egos. And in a Christian's life and ministry, there is no room for this kind of practice. Christ is the only one to be exalted while we are to be diminished. Then and only then will God be glorified before men. So again, keep your rider considerably simple.

I hope by now you understand the importance of having a contract and rider (if needed) when booking ministry opportunities. For your convenience, the following are tips to remember when writing a contract/rider:

- **Don't Reinvent the Wheel.** There are templates on the web and in books (that will guide you through the process. Regardless of which source you use to draft your contract, please have an attorney or experienced artist manager to review it.

- **Keep it Simple.** Only include the essential details such as date, time, place, name, and address of hosting organization, performance criteria (i.e., number of songs) honorarium amount, travel detail, and a technical and professional rider. Remember, the ministry is not about you but Christ. So don't make it about you when drafting your rider. Keep it Christ-centered.

- **Consult with an Attorney.** Seek legal advice before signing ANY contract. The goal is to make sure you haven't left any *important* details out or *unwanted* details in.

- **Act Like the Professional that You Are.** If for no other reason, writing a contract is just professional and helps to ensure excellence in what you do (Titus 2:7). Furthermore, it draws a clearly defined line between the performance and the business. And believe me when I say your ministry is God's business. So treat it like it is!

- **Once Signed, Enforce It.** There is nothing that reveals a lack of integrity in a person than a broken promise or agreement. As believers, we are to hold each other accountable. Therefore, make sure that you and the other party in the agreement uphold their end of the deal. Anything less would not only be dishonorable to each other, but to God.

MINISTRY CHECK

It is always difficult to discuss money and ministry outside of the required tithe and offering. Even after being in ministry for over two decades, I still find myself hesitant to state my honorarium and contract terms—that is why I have a manager. Maybe it's due to the fact that I was raised in a church that frowned upon paying for gospel music. Maybe, it was due to the haggling I experienced one time too many to receive decent pay for a ministry I have invested my heart, soul, time, and money to achieve and maintain a level of excellence. After all, that is what God requires of all who serve Him. Or maybe it's because I respect and understand the importance and seriousness of my calling, and don't want anyone to mistake my asking for an honorarium to mean that I am doing it for the money, not ministry.

Regardless of the reason, I know it is important to know why I do what I do and that I have the right to fair compensation for doing it. But with that said, let me be clear about one thing. Pay or no pay, at the end of the day, and my life, it has and always will be about the mission— edifying the church and recruiting souls for Christ!

135

What about you? Where is your focus in ministry? Is it centered in Christ?

MINISTRY CHALLENGE

Honestly answer the following questions to determine if you need a makeover for the business element of your ministry:

- Do you believe ministry has a business element?

- Do you struggle with handling the business side of ministry?

- Are you comfortable asking for an honorarium?

- How do you calculate your honorarium? Are your fees fair and realistic?

- Is your honorarium meeting your needs?

- Do you use a contract/rider? If you haven't in the past, do you now see the importance of using one?

- Would you benefit from outsourcing the management of your ministry?

The above questions are what you must answer if you desire and need monetary compensation for your service in ministry. Again, regardless of what people think or say, it is okay to receive pay! For it is both biblical and justifiable. Remember, you are not selling the Gospel, but funding the cause. And they are not buying the message but financially supporting the messenger. So be confident in knowing that you are in the will of God, and be about *the mission!*

> **NOTE:** *If you are not comfortable handling the business side of your ministry, recruit a qualified person to help while you focus on what you do best...minister!*

OUTRO

He put a new song in my mouth, a hymn of praise to our God. Many will see and fear the Lord and put their trust in him. (Psalms 40:3, NIV)

Wow! I can't believe we are already at the end of the book. I would never have guessed that I would be an author of a book about Christian ministry. God sure is full of pleasant surprises!

I must say that it has been quite a journey for me while writing this book. Every word written on the pages has reminded me of my responsibility as a Christian artist, as well as revitalized my commitment to and relationship with God. I hope and pray that it has done the same for you.

Yes, there were some rather tough things to swallow within this book, if you were totally honest with yourself. But I truly believe that God wouldn't have it any other way.

He only wants what's best for you. And that is for you to live in His *perfect* will which includes eternal life.

Like Peter (if I can go back to the example mention in the introduction of this book), if you find yourself sinking under the waves of self-exaltation, self-satisfaction or any other "self" derived motive or desire, quickly look to Jesus, confess your sin and take His hand. Let Him lead you safely back into His will for your life...your ministry.

I know sometimes our past can weigh us down with guilt and shame, leading us to believe the enemy's lie that God can't use us because we have gone too deep in sin or we have been a hypocrite so long in ministry. But it is just that—a lie! So stop believing it, and rebuke it instead. Then with the power of the Holy Spirit within you, *MOVE FORWARD!*

Right now, I need you to recite Isaiah 43:18-19a, *"Remember ye not the former things, neither consider the things of old. 19 Behold, I will do a new thing."* Now believe it, and claim it, for it is God's precious promise to you.

Well, it's time for me to wrap this up! But before I do, I want you to do one last thing. Close your eyes and imagine what the future holds for you should you decide to do things God's way. Perfect peace, unspeakable joy, life-fulfilling purpose and many more blessings await you. The Bible says the Father withholds no good thing from those who love and obey Him (Ps. 84:11). I know first-hand what God can do with little when placed in His powerful hands. Your life will *never* be the same. Mine isn't. And I thank God for it!

In closing, having a music ministry, where I aim to keep Christ the center of attention, is an honor and a blessing. Every word I write, speak, or sing reminds me of a loving God and Savior who wants nothing but the best for me, *so much so* that He gave His life for me! And one day, if I stay faithful to Him, I will see Him face-to-face and never again will sin enslave me. *Hallelujah!* And the good news is He's done the same for you!

So what are you waiting for? Let Christ take you and your music (or whatever) ministry to a level that only He can accomplish.

MINISTRY CHECK

You've read the book in its entirety (at least I hope you did). Now the question is, "how does your ministry measure up according to this book's checks and challenges?" The more important question is, "what are you going to do with the information you received?"

MINISTRY CHALLENGE

As your final "ministry challenge," right now, decide to make and keep Christ center stage in your ministry and your life. If, after prayerfully reading this book, you are convicted by the Holy Spirit that elements of your ministry need to change so that it reflects Christ and Christ alone, then make it your mission to make the necessary changes. I am confident that with the aid of the Holy Spirit, your music ministry will not only lift-up the name of Jesus, but it will also draw all men unto Him. Not only will your audience be blessed, but you will too.

I do have one "personal challenge" for you. Because I *know* God is going to *blow* your mind as He begins revamping your ministry, I challenge you to share with me what you experience. It would be a huge blessing to me from you.

To share how God is revamping both your music ministry and life, please feel free to contact me at:

msangelabryant@gmail.com

or post a comment at:

www.facebook.com/sounds4thesoul

www.sounds4thesoul.com.

I look forward to your comments and thank you in advance.

As you move forward in your ministry, may God richly bless you for **_Keeping Christ Center Stage!_**

Sacred Space:

Please use the following pages to jot down your thoughts, "ah-ha" moments, and epiphanies.

Chapter 1

Chapter 2

Chapter 3

Chapter 4

Chapter 5

Chapter 6

Chapter 7

Chapter 8

About the Author

For Angela L. Bryant, praise and worship is more than a style of music. It is what she does in response to God's presence in her life.

Her passion for worship has led her to become a vibrant worship leader, prolific songwriter, recording artist, producer of three CD recordings, *From You, A Song in the Air,* and *In Hymn I Trust,* and recently the author of *Keeping Christ Center Stage* and the children's book, *Tell Me.*

A native of Syracuse, New York, Bryant recognized her call to music ministry at the age of 7. Since Bryant's call to ministry, she's been very active in ministry for various kinds of public/private events to include worship services, retreats, weddings, and solo concerts, to name a few.

In 2005, Bryant established the ministry, *Sounds 4 the Soul,* providing inspirational, uplifting music and spoken word for its listeners. In 2006, she founded the non-profit organization, *By Your Side Ministries,* which provides educational support to single-teen parents. Three years later Bryant hosted her internet radio talk show, *Life Happens: Now What?*

In 2012, Bryant officially launched her speaking career. Organizations that have featured her as their keynote speaker, describes her presentation as "inspiring", "empowering", and "absolutely captivating". Bryant consistently exceeds her listeners' expectations with her full-of-life, thought-provoking presentations often culminated with a compelling song to reinforce the message.

Bryant considers herself a living testimony of what God can do for those who love and trust Him with their whole heart. When asked what her message is, Bryant says, "Successful living is living within God's will." As stated in one of her songs:

"For you were born with a purpose, perfectly designed,
when God breathed life into you, He had a purpose in mind!

To invite Angela L. Bryant to sing, speak, or facilitate a music workshop at your upcoming event, or to purchase her music and other merchandise, please contact the office of *Sounds4theSoul* at:

Office: 703.314.2990
Email: Angela@sounds4thesoul.com
www.sounds4thesoul.com

We look forward to serving you!

Made in the USA
Middletown, DE
19 March 2022

62838831R00102